Cooking
with
Gluten
and
Seitan

by Dorothy R. Bates
and Colby Wingate

The Book Publishing Company
Summertown, Tennessee

Cover and interior design by Barbara McNew
Cover photo by Thomas Johns

Library of Congress Cataloging-in-Publication Data
Bates, Dorothy R., 1921-
Cooking with gluten and seitan / by Dorothy R. Bates
and Colby Wingate.
p. cm.
Includes index.
ISBN 0-913990-95-7
1. Cookery (Gluten) I. Title II. Wingate, Colby.
III. Title: Cooking with gluten and seitan.
TX809.G55B38   1993
641.6'311—dc20   92-44423

CIP

ISBN 0-913990-95-7

0 9 8 7 6 5 4 3

Calculations for the nutritional analyses in this book are based on the
average number of servings listed with the recipes and the average
amount of an ingredient if a range is called for. Calculations are
rounded up to the nearest gram. If two options for an ingredient are
listed, the first one is used. Not included are fat used for frying, unless
the amount is specified in the recipe, optional ingredients, or servings suggestions.

TABLE OF CONTENTS

INTRODUCTION

Technically, the name seitan is a Japanese term meaning "gluten cooked in a soy sauce broth." Cooked gluten has been a traditional food among Buddhists for hundreds of years. Often called "wheat meat," it's been popular with vegetarians in this country for several decades. To celebrate feast days, holidays and weddings vegetarians and vegans often prepare and serve a large gluten roast. It wasn't made more often because of the many hours it took to rinse the starch from the flour by hand to make the gluten.

Today instant gluten flour (vital wheat gluten) makes it possible to prepare and serve roasts, loaves and other gluten dishes frequently. **Don't confuse instant gluten flour with high gluten wheat flour often sold in health food or speciality stores for use in baking. They're not the same product and won't give you the same results.** Liquid is added to instant gluten flour (basically dried powdered gluten), reconstituting it into a stiff dough which is then cooked. Instant gluten flour keeps indefinitely in the refrigerator as long as it's kept dry. The cooked gluten or seitan will keep several days in the refrigerator and many months in the freezer, so seitan can be a menu mainstay any time.

Many natural food stores sell packaged seitan or cooked gluten in jars, cans, boxes and as frozen food. Some of these items have been imported from Japan but a growing number are made right here in the United States. These will vary in flavor, some being on the salty side, and will also vary in texture from a little spongy to very firm. As the ready-to-serve seitan tends to be rather expensive, we hope this book will encourage you to make your own so you can enjoy this healthful food often.

Recipes handed down through generations are part of our rich cultural American heritage. These recipes originated "in the old country" and have been adapted by American ingenuity to please appetites today. Seitan lends itself beautifully to a wide variety of these ethnic recipes, and we've tried to capture that "old world" flavor in recipes included in this book.

Dorothy R. Bates and Colby Wingate

A Word About Nutrition

The connection between what we eat and how long we live is becoming clear as our understanding of diet and health increases. Cancer and heart disease kill more people and cause more pain and suffering than any other ailments, and more and more research confirms the link between diet and these diseases. A change to healthy eating habits is not that difficult to do, and experimenting with a new and healthy way of eating can be an adventure.

Dr. Dean Ornish, M.D., director of the Preventive Medicine Research Institute at the University of California, launched a study in 1986 to determine the effects of comprehensive life-style changes on patients with severe cardiovascular disease. The patients in the study group agreed to switch to a vegetarian diet, exercise daily and practice yoga and meditation to reduce stress. An amazing 82% of the patients who embarked on these changes had a measurable *reversal* of coronary artery blockages; not just a slow-down in the progression of the disease but an actual reversal! In contrast, cardiovascular disease progressed in members of the control group, as they followed standard treatment for heart disease and did not make drastic changes in their diets or life styles.

Research also shows a link between diet and cancer. In a recent five year study in Sweden, one group of men was placed on a diet high in fiber and low in fat, while those in the control group ate their usual diet. No man in the high fiber, low fat group got cancer while several in the control group were diagnosed with colon, prostate or rectal cancer during the study.

The important thing to remember is that **there is no cholesterol in the plant kingdom** It exists only in the animal kingdom. And **there is no fiber in the animal kingdom**. Fiber (what our parents used to call "roughage") can be found in whole grains, legumes, vegetables and fruits. A delicious, healthy diet can be built around these foods.

Gluten/seitan contains some of the complex carbohydrates that raise body metabolism while providing a good source of protein. There is no cholesterol in gluten and very little fat although most of our recipes add a little fat to maximize flavor. If you are on a slimming program, instead of sautéing the onions, garlic, peppers, etc. in oil at the start of a recipe, omit the oil and soften them by simmering in a little water for a few minutes. Any excess calories one consumes as fat are easily stored in the body as fat but excess calories taken in as complex carbohydrates are not stored as fat as easily.

Making Gluten

**Gluten (the protein of wheat) is uncooked seitan.
Seitan is gluten that has been cooked (traditionally in
a soy sauce broth).**

Let's take a look at the various ways you can make gluten, then transform it into seitan:

Making gluten from scratch

The time-honored way to make raw gluten (which many still like to do today) is by mixing wheat flour and water into a ball of dough, and letting it rest for 30 minutes to an hour to develop the gluten. Then the dough is gently rinsed and kneaded under water to wash away the starch and the bran from the flour until only the gluten or the protein of the flour remains.

The kneading and rinsing process can be done on and off for half a day or be done in one to two hours. The starchy water and the bran that are removed can be saved and used in a variety of ways if one cares to take the trouble. The flour used must have a high gluten content; refined white "cake" flour or whole wheat pastry flour that makes a fine cake would not make good gluten. Professional gluten makers prefer organic whole wheat flour; some like hard winter wheat, others hard spring wheat. Unbleached white flour has a high gluten content and many cooks mix it half and half with whole wheat flour.

If you prefer to make your gluten using this method, you can use the following recipe:

> **5 cups hard red spring wheat flour
>   (or wheat flour of your choice)
> 2½ cups warm water**

Place flour in a large bowl and add water. Mix to form a wet, smooth dough. With the dough still in the bowl, knead with wet hands or mix about 100 times to develop the gluten.

Cover the dough with lukewarm water for 15-30 minutes, then pour water off and replace with cold water. Place the large bowl of dough in your kitchen sink. Gently at first and then more vigorously, knead and stretch the dough under the water. This will release the starch into the water, turning it milky and leaving the gluten (grey and stretchy) in the bowl. Carefully pour off the starchy water once it becomes white and fill the bowl with more cold water. Knead and rinse until the water is almost clear (about three or more times).

You may find that halfway through the kneading process there comes a point where the dough seems to be dissolving. Keep pressing what pieces of dough are left back into themselves. Eventually enough of the starch is rinsed out that the remaining gluten holds together on its own. Feel for any gritty parts where the bran is left and rinse those out. The rinsing process takes about 10 to 20 minutes. Your finished gluten is then ready for processing into seitan. This recipe will make about 12 ounces or 3 cups of cooked seitan.

Making gluten quickly with instant gluten flour (vital wheat gluten)

Instant gluten flour has already had the starch and bran removed and needs only to be mixed with seasoning and liquid. You can use the following recipe to make about 24 oz. or 6 cups of seitan, enough to use in about 3 or 4 of the recipes in this book:

> **2 cups instant gluten flour**
> **1½ - 1¾ cups liquid**

It's a good idea to first measure any dry seasonings you'd like to use into a mixing bowl and stir them together well. Then thoroughly mix the seasonings with the dry instant gluten flour using a whisk or fork. Seasonings that go well with gluten are garlic and onion powder, chili powder, oregano, thyme and nutritional yeast. Experiment with different combinations and amounts according to what you'll be making with the finished seitan.

In another bowl, measure the liquid, usually broth or water plus soy sauce or miso, and perhaps a little oil. You can also combine the liquid in a blender with chopped onion, green pepper or other flavorful vegetables. (This is a good way to get these ingredients into your gluten without alerting your children!) Combine the wet and dry ingredients quickly, using a fork or spoon to stir, then knead with your hands into a smooth ball, adding another spoonful or two of liquid if needed. It takes almost as much liquid as dry ingredients to make the raw gluten dough; too much liquid can yield a soggy product. The dough is then cooked in stock to become seitan (see page 10).

One cup of instant gluten flour, simmered in liquid and drained, yields 12 ounces or about 3 cups of seitan that can be prepared in a number of ways.

Instant gluten flour can be ordered directly from

The Mail Order Catalog, P.O. Box 180, Summertown, TN 38483. (1-800-695-2241)

COOKING GLUTEN TO MAKE SEITAN

Even though the word "seitan" means gluten cooked in a soy sauce or tamari broth, it has come to mean any cooked gluten. Soy sauce in the cooking water helps to keep the cooked gluten (seitan) fresh for several days. The cooking liquid can be clear spring water to which soy sauce, sea vegetables and perhaps gingerroot are added, or it can be a vegetable broth plus a spoonful of soy sauce. Various cooking methods give different textures to the seitan. It is worth experimenting to find what method suits your palate best. The many ways to turn gluten into seitan include simmering, baking, braising, water bath and pressure cooking. Once cooked it will keep for 3 to 5 days in the refrigerator, stored in a covered dish, or for months in the freezer.

1. Simmering

Once the raw gluten has been prepared by mixing instant gluten flour with liquid, it is then shaped and cooked in a flavorful broth for 45-50 minutes. As it simmers the gluten will absorb some of the liquid and flavors. A general rule of thumb on the amount of cooking liquid to use is two to three times as much liquid as you have gluten. Sea vegetables, such as kombu, wakame, arame or hijiki, can be added to the cooking water (1 tsp. or a 1" piece per cup), plus soy sauce (about 1½ Tablespoons per cup) and pieces of gingerroot (a 1" piece per cup. The broth that is left after cooking can be thickened and seasoned for sauce or gravy to serve with the seitan.

The gluten can be cooked in one long roll, or it can be broken off into balls and stretched into cutlets or medallions to simmer (See **BASIC SEITAN**, pg. 12). A large ball of gluten can be cut up into small cubes before simmering.

2. Water bath cooking

Making up raw gluten, packing it into lightly oiled cans and cooking it in a water bath is another excellent method. It produces a firm seitan "roll" that is easily sliced and freezes very well. Flavors can be varied, so you could prepare several types of gluten with different flavorings and water bath them in one batch. One can might contain a breakfast sausage roll to slice for patties, one a spicy Spanish flavored roll, one a plainer mixture for grinding and perhaps (in a small juice can) an Italian pepperoni for pizza.

3. Baking as a loaf

Gluten can also be baked in a loaf pan, covered with liquid (most of which it will absorb in the baking process). See **BAKED GLUTEN LOAF**, pg. 15.

4. Braising as a pot roast

Shaped like a large oval roast and placed in a covered roaster with plenty of liquid, gluten makes an excellent seitan pot roast. Vegetables can be added for a one dish meal. See **POT ROAST**, pg. 13.

5. Baking for grinding

Ground seitan is handy to have on hand and is used in a number of recipes in this book. One way to get a lot to grind or process is to spread a batch of raw gluten out on a lightly oiled cookie sheet, stretching and pulling it to flatten out as thin as possible. Bake it for an hour at a moderate temperature (350°) then grind the dry seitan in a blender or food processor for 20-30 seconds. If it becomes too dry and hard, break it up and soak in water to soften for grinding. Ground seitan keeps very well in a plastic bag in a freezer and defrosts quickly.

6. Combining "bake and simmer" method

Little balls or flat dollops of the uncooked gluten can be dropped on a lightly oiled baking sheet, baked for 20 minutes in a moderate oven (350°), until they are lightly browned and puffy, then dropped into a broth to simmer for 35 minutes. See **SAUSAGE PATTIES**, pg. 39.

7. Pressure Cooking

Many cooks prefer pressure cooking gluten to save time and feel this method makes very good seitan. Make up about 2 cups of raw gluten (1 cup instant gluten flour + ⅞ cup water). Place in a broth made with 6 cups water and ¼ cup soy sauce (a 6" piece of sea vegetable and 1" of fresh gingerroot cut up are optional additions). Cook under 15 lbs. pressure for 45 minutes. Let the pressure come down by itself or cool the pressure cooker by placing it in a sinkful of cold water.

8. Brown Bits for topping

Don't overlook "brown bits" that can be made from simmered or braised seitan. For **fried brown bits**, heat a skillet and add 1 Tablespoon sesame oil. Tilt pan to coat. Add 1 cup seitan torn off into very small bits or diced small. Stir fry 3 to 5 minutes over medium high heat until bits turn lightly brown. Keep the bits covered and refrigerated until ready to use.

Baked bits can be made in a toaster oven. Arrange a cup of finely diced or ground seitan in a single layer on a lightly oiled pan and bake at 350° for 12-14 minutes, stirring half way through. To microwave, spread out in a layer on a lightly oiled flat plate and microwave on high power 5 to 7 minutes, turning and stirring once.

These "bits" add nutrition, flavor and crunch to a variety of recipes from **Fried Rice,** pg. 55, and **Stuffed Peppers,** pg. 105, to warm spinach or potato salad.

The following three recipes are good examples of basic ways to transform gluten into seitan. They are delicious by themselves and will provide you with a quantity of seitan to use in the other recipes in this book.

Basic Gluten

Makes 4 servings (12 oz. or 3 cups seitan)

Stir together thoroughly in a bowl:
    1 cup instant gluten flour (vital wheat gluten)
    ⅞ cup water or vegetable stock

Knead a minute a minute to blend. Divide into 16 to 20 balls, stretching and pressing to flatten into cutlets.

Drop the gluten cutlets into:
    6 cups vegetable stock

Cover the pan and bring the stock to a simmer. Reduce the heat to very low and simmer the cutlets gently for about 50 minutes. Drain and cool before using.

Per Serving: Calories: 103, Protein: 28 gm., Carbohydrates: 5 gm., Fat: 1 gm.

POT ROAST WITH VEGETABLES

8 to 10 servings

See photo on cover.
An old-fashioned hearty meal with a tantalizing aroma as it cooks. Leftover pot roast is excellent to slice, cube or grind for other recipes.

Stir together thoroughly in a 2 quart bowl:
   2 cups instant gluten flour
   2 Tablespoons nutritional yeast
   1 teaspoon onion powder (optional)
   ½ teaspoon garlic powder
   ⅛ teaspoon black pepper

Measure into another bowl:
   1½ cups warm water
   2 Tablespoons olive oil
   2 Tablespoons soy sauce

Mix wet and dry ingredients together all at once, adding a spoonful or two of water if all the dry ingredients are not moistened. Knead a minute to blend and shape into an oval loaf. Lightly oil the bottom of a large oven roasting pan that has a tight fitting cover. Place gluten in roasting pan.

Preheat oven to 350° and mix for the cooking broth:
   5 cups water
   2 Tablespoons olive oil
   2 Tablespoons soy sauce

Pour broth over the gluten and cook uncovered for 30 minutes. If gluten puffs up, prick with a fork all over the top. Remove from oven and carefully turn the roast over. Surround with:
   8 potatoes, cut in quarters
   6 carrots, cut in 2" chunks
   3 medium onions, cut in halves

Baste the vegetables with the pan liquids, cover the roasting pan, return to oven and bake 1 hour more, basting roast and vegetables once or twice during the cooking time. Remove roast to a platter and surround with vegetables.

To thicken the cooking liquid for gravy, mix:
    1 Tablespoon arrowroot
    2 Tablespoons cold water

Slowly add 2-3 cups cooking liquid, cooking and stirring until it thickens and bubbles.

Per Serving: Calories: 296, Protein: 32 gm., Carbohydrates: 34 gm., Fat: 7 gm.

BASIC BAKED GLUTEN LOAF

18 to 20 slices

This makes a large loaf suitable for a holiday feast. This recipes can easily be doubled for leftovers and used for cutting into thin strips for Chinese recipes or small cubes to use in other recipes. You can also cut the loaf into chunks and whiz in a processor for recipes that call for ground seitan, like stuffed peppers, pizza, chili or fried rice.

Measure into a bowl and mix these dry ingredients well with a whisk:

> 3 cups instant gluten flour
> ½ cup whole wheat or unbleached flour
> 2 Tablespoons nutritional yeast
> 1 teaspoon marjoram
> 1 teaspoon thyme
> 1 teaspoon salt

Heat a skillet and add:

> ¼ cup oil

When oil is hot, stir in:

> 1 cup onions, coarsely chopped

Cook slowly, about 10 minutes, until onions are tender. Purée the onions in a blender, adding:

> ¼ cup soy sauce
> 2 Tablespoons catsup or tomato paste
> 2 cups warm water

Pour the blender liquids into the dry ingredients while stirring quickly, adding a little more water if needed to moisten the flour. Gluten will be firm. Knead for a minute, then press into a lightly oiled 9"x 5"x 3" loaf pan. Two smaller pans can be used, but allow space for the sauce and reduce cooking time.

Preheat oven to 350°. Mix for baking sauce:

> 1 Tablespoon catsup or tomato paste
> 1 Tablespoon soy sauce
> 1 cup water or stock

Pour sauce over top of loaf and bake 60 minutes. Decrease heat to 325° and bake 30 minutes more. Almost all of the liquid will be absorbed by the loaf. If it begins to dry out too soon, pour a little stock on top of loaf and cover pan with aluminum foil. The loaf will slice easier if allowed to cool for 10 minutes. To serve, lift loaf onto a platter, garnish with sprigs of parsley and thin lemon slices.

If you make the loaf the day before, reheat by placing the loaf pan in a shallow pan of hot water, cover the pan and bake at 350° for 30-40 minutes. To reheat on top of stove, use a deep skillet or pan with a cover and simmer loaf still in the baking pan over low heat about 40 minutes to heat through.

Per Serving: Calories: 118, Protein: 20 gm., Carbohydrates: 8 gm., Fat: 3 gm.

INGREDIENTS

Water is the most important ingredient in making your own seitan. It is used copiously throughout the rinsing process, if you make your own raw gluten. It is used to transform instant gluten flour into the gluten that will cook into seitan. It is used for the cooking water or broth that the gluten soaks up while simmering. If you have city water that is heavy in chemicals, we suggest you use bottled springwater to make the gluten and the broth. Other ingredients we have used in these recipes include:

Arrowroot: a powder made from the roots of a nutritive plant, serves as a thickening agent. Dissolve in a little cold water before stirring into a sauce.

Barley malt syrup: a thick dark sweetener made from sprouted grains.

Basmati rice (brown): we use the long grained brown basmati rice that has a delicious, nutty flavor. It is available at natural food stores.

Bulgur: cracked wheat, hulled and parboiled to use a grain or as a substitute for rice.

Capers: the flower buds of a shrub that grows near the Mediterranean. These are pickled when you buy them; a few will add interesting flavor to sauces, salads and casseroles.

Couscous: refined from semolina, the heart of the wheat kernel, to create small, golden grains that fluff up when steamed.

Daikon radish: a long white radish used in Japanese cooking.

Dried soy bean curd: see *Yuba*

Mirin: a liquid made from cultured rice, it has a slightly sweet flavor. White wine or white grape juice can be substituted.

Miso: a fermented food product made from soybeans, salt, water and a starter culture called *koji*. Miso is also made with barley, chick peas and other ingredients. It is usually a thick paste and comes in several flavors and colors, ranging from pale to dark brown, depending on length of aging. It is considered an aid to digestion, is rich in lactic acid-forming bacteria and is a high quality protein food. When making a sauce, add miso last to keep the beneficial enzymes intact, and never let it boil. Thin the miso paste with a little water, then slowly stir it into the simmering broth near the end of the cooking time. Miso may be salty, so taste as you go.

Nutritional yeast *(saccharomyces cerevisiae)*: a good tasting yeast grown in a molasses solution. It contain all the amino acids and is a good source of B vitamins (B12 is occasionally added by the manufacturer). Its riboflavin content lends it a gold or yellow color. It is 40% protein and only ½% fat. See the recipe for "Cheeze Sauce" on page 109 made with nutritional yeast.

Oils: we have used olive oil (high in monounsaturated fats) and safflower oil (high in polyunsaturated fats). Also, both light sesame oil which is rather bland and the dark toasted sesame oil that is rich in flavor.

Pine nuts: the seeds from cones of certain pine trees are also called pignolias or pinyons. Toasting brings out their flavor.

Sea vegetables: such as kombu, hijiki and wakame are used to flavor the broth for cooking gluten, kombu being the one that is least likely to fall into pieces. These sea products are excellent sources of A, E and B vitamins and have been found to remove radioactive strontium-90 from the body.

Soy sauce: See *Tamari*.

Sun-dried tomatoes: relatively new to the market and great to have on hand. Soften them in hot water, and slice or chop to add flavor and color to many dishes. These can also be purchased soaking in olive oil, but this kind is high in fat.

Tahini: a thick paste of ground sesame seeds that adds flavor, protein and calcium to recipes. If the oil separates out, stir it in with a fork.

Tamari: use a naturally aged shoyu or a tamari with no color or preservatives added. Read the label before you purchase one. If you're on a yeast-free diet, try Bragg's Liquid Aminos, an unfermented product.

Umeboshi plum: actually a type of Japanese apricot, soaked in brine and sun-dried repeatedly. It is reputed to have the ability to stop food from going bad and adds a salty, tart flavor to salad dressings, cooked vegetables or sauces.

Vegetable stock: easily made with cubes or powders sold in natural food stores. Morga® is a good brand and has a low fat content.

Yuba: the Japanese name for dried soy bean curd, which is actually the film that forms on top of heated soy milk. It comes in flat light brown sheets that will keep indefinitely but can shatter if not handled gently. Soaking in water softens the sheets and makes them flexible enough to use as wrapping. See the recipe for TURKEY ROLL, pg. 51.

Recipes

Empanadas

20 turnovers

Every country has its version of meat-filled turnovers. This is a vegetarian version of a Chilean recipe. The filling is customarily wrapped in a flaky pastry crust but to minimize fat (and time) we used a commercial biscuit dough.

Have ready:
> **4 ounces seitan, diced small (1 cup)**
> **1 cup onions, chopped**
> **2-3 jalapeño peppers, minced**
> **2 (12 oz.) cans commercial biscuit dough***

Heat a pan, tilting to coat bottom while adding:
> **1 Tablespoon olive oil**

Add the onions and peppers to the oil and cook over medium low heat about 10 minutes.

Stir into the diced seitan:
> **1 teaspoon oregano**   **½ teaspoon chili oil or hot sauce**
> **1 teaspoon paprika**   **pinch of salt**

Add the seitan to the onions, fry 2 minutes and stir in:
> **¼ cup ripe or stuffed olives, chopped**
> **3 Tablespoons raisins**

Set filling aside. You will have a scant 3 cups.

Preheat oven to 400°. Roll out 20 biscuits on a floured work surface, rolling each to ⅛ inch thick and 5 inches in diameter. Place a heaping tablespoon of filling in each circle and fold in half. Pinch the edges together or press edges with a fork to seal. Place on lightly oiled baking sheets and bake for 8 to 10 minutes. Reduce heat to 375° if they are browning too much. You may want to switch trays on upper and lower oven shelves after 5 minutes. Remove to a cooling rack and if you like, lightly brush tops with a little bit of oil to give crust a lovely shine.

* To make your own biscuit dough combine in the following order: 3 cups of flour, 3 tsp. baking powder, ½ tsp salt, ⅓ cup oil, and ⅔ cup soymilk

Per Empanada: Calories: 98, Protein: 5 gm., Carbohydrates: 15 gm., Fat: 2 gm.

STUFFED MUSHROOMS

12 mushrooms

Mushrooms are full of flavor as well as vitamins and minerals,
and there are only 90 calories in a whole pound.
These can be served as an appetizer or an entrée.

Clean by wiping with a damp cloth:
12 large mushrooms

Break off the stems and trim off ends before chopping, setting the whole caps aside.

Heat a skillet and add:
2 teaspoons olive oil
2 green onions, chopped fine
the chopped mushroom stems

Sauté for 3 minutes, then stir in:
½ cup bread crumbs
½ cup ground seitan
1 teaspoon marjoram
¼ teaspoon garlic powder
dash of salt and pepper

Cook for 2 minutes, mixing well. Pack filling in cavities of mushroom caps. Brush skillet lightly with oil and place caps around bottom, filled side up. Let the caps brown for a minute, reduce heat and add to the bottom of the pan:
½ cup stock

Cover pan and simmer 20 minutes. Or place stuffed caps in a lightly oiled baking pan, add stock and bake uncovered at 375° for 15-20 minutes.

As an entrée:

Stuffed mushrooms are excellent served on a bed of cooked young mustard greens or kale.

Strip the tender leaves and discard stems from:
1 pound mustard greens or kale

Wash well, rinse and pat dry. Take several leaves, roll up into a bundle and slice each bundle thinly. Drop shreds into a large pot of boiling water, cook until just barely tender and drain.

In another pan sauté until heated through:
> **2 teaspoons olive oil**
> **1 clove garlic, minced**

Toss with the hot drained greens. Arrange greens in a circle on each plate and top with 3 stuffed mushrooms for each entrée.

As an appetizer (Per Mushroom): Calories: 32, Protein: 2 gm., Carbohydrates: 4 gm., Fat: 1 gm.

As an entrée (Per 3 Mushrooms): Calories: 156, Protein: 11 gm., Carbohydrates: 19 gm., Fat: 5 gm.

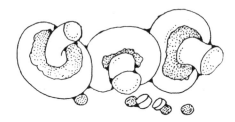

PÂTÉ

Makes 24 ounces

This makes a large amount, enough for the PÂTÉ EN BAGUETTE recipe (pg. 26) or to pack into several small jars and give to friends. It can also be spread on melba toast rounds or crackers and would serve 24 as a spread.

Have ready:
8 oz. ground seitan (about 2 cups)

Cut thin slices of rind with a vegetable peeler, then cut into small slivers and set aside:
1 lemon

Place in a mixing bowl:
1 quart dry bread cubes (day-old bread or toast)

Pour over bread and let soak:
½ cup vegetable stock

Heat a pan and sauté (or place in a glass bowl if using the microwave):
1 Tablespoon olive oil
1 medium onion, chopped

When onion is soft, mix with the bread and seitan, adding:
the slivered lemon rind
1 teaspoon marjoram
1 teaspoon QUATRE EPICES (see page 85)
½ teaspoon salt
⅛ teaspoon lemon pepper

Mixture should be moist but not mushy. Add a little more broth if it seems dry.

For cooking in a microwave, line a pyrex loaf pan (8" x 5" x 3") with plastic wrap, leaving a 4" overhang. Pack in the seitan mixture, pressing down. Cover with the overhanging plastic. Microwave on high for 10 minutes, rotate pan halfway around (if microwave has no turntable) and microwave 5 minutes more.

If baking in the oven, preheat oven to 350°. Line pan and cover pâté with foil, and place loaf pan in a pan of hot water. Bake for 45-50 minutes.

After pâté is cooked, let cool. Cut out a piece of cardboard to fit on top of the loaf, weight the cardboard down with two heavy cans and chill pâté overnight. Unmold. It will keep for several days in the refrigerator.

Per Ounce: Calories: 91, Protein: 7 gm., Carbohydrates: 14 gm., Fat: 1 gm.,

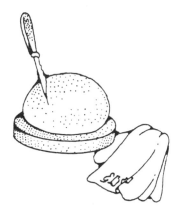

PÂTÉ EN BAGUETTE

50 slices

A delightful variation on the traditional, very elegant and very fattening pâté en croute, this surrounds the pâté with bread instead of flaky pastry.

Cut in half lengthwise:
> **1 (30-34" long) whole wheat French baguette**

Hollow out each half, using a knife to cut strips from the centers and leaving about ½" thick shell within the crusts. The leftover bread can be used in making the pâté or whizzed in a blender for crumbs.

To prepare in a microwave, heat for 30 seconds in a glass bowl:
> **2 teaspoons olive oil**
> **2 garlic cloves, chopped**

Add to bowl and cover with plastic:
> **1 large sweet red pepper, cut in thin strips**

Heat in microwave on full power for about 3 minutes, stirring once. Cool.

For top-of-stove cooking, place pepper strips in a sauce pan with a cup of water, cover pan and simmer 5 to 10 minutes until tender. Drain and mix with the olive oil and garlic.

Have ready:
> **3 Tablespoons fresh basil or parsley, minced**

Sprinkle the insides of the baguette shells with the minced herbs. Pack each half with the cooked pâté, heaping up the pâté some in the middle and pressing down to remove any air bubbles. Lay the pepper strips on top of the pâté for the length of one side of the loaf. Press the top half on the bottom half of the loaf and wrap tightly in plastic wrap. Chill overnight. Slice the chilled loaf on the diagonal to make attractive elliptical ½" slices.

For a first course, serve 3 slices on a bed of endive and garnish the plate with a cherry tomato cut in wedges.

Per Slice: Calories: 61, Protein: 4 gm., Carbohydrates: 10 gm., Fat: 1 gm.

CRICK'S HOMEMADE CHILI

Serves 4

My husband's wonderful vegetarian chili!

Sauté in a medium pan until transparent:
- **1 medium onion, chopped**
- **1 rib celery, minced**
- **1 small bell pepper, chopped**
- **1 tablespoon corn oil**
- **2 cloves garlic, minced**

Add and simmer on low heat for 20-30 minutes:
- **2 cups water**
- **1 cup cooked kidney beans**
- **1 (8 oz.) can whole tomatoes**
  - **or 2-3 medium fresh tomatoes, chopped**
- **2 tablespoons tomato paste**
- **1 tablespoon chili powder**
- **1 cup vegetable broth**

Chop finely by hand or grind in a blender or food processor for 20-30 seconds:
- **8 oz. seitan**

Add seitan to the chili and simmer 10 minutes more, adjusting seasonings if necessary. Add more water if needed to achieve desired consistency.

Serve piping hot.

Per Serving: Calories: 195, Protein: 24 gm., Carbohydrates: 22 gm., Fat: 4 gm.

Rich Split Pea Soup

Serves 4 to 6

You can vary this soup by using other vegetables, such as turnips, potatoes and celery. A touch of fresh or dried basil is a nice change.

Bring to a boil in a 4 quart pot:

6 cups water
1 cup vegetable broth
1 (3") strip kombu (optional)

Add, lower heat and simmer 40 minutes, or until creamy:

2 cups dried split peas
2 medium carrots, diced
1 medium onion, diced

Add and simmer 5-10 minutes:

8 oz. seitan, cubed
tamari to taste

Stir in:

2 tablespoons miso dissolved in 3 tablespoons water

If you're using kombu and it didn't dissolve in the cooking process, remove from pot, cut in small squares and add to soup. Garnish soup with fresh parsley and serve.

Per Serving: Calories: 189, Protein: 23 gm., Carbohydrates: 28 gm., Fat: 1 gm.

MINESTRONE

12 servings (about 3 quarts)

A thick soup brimming with colorful vegetables, savory and satisfying, this takes little preparation time. The tiny pasta used here is called orzo in Greece (or pastina in Italy).

Heat a 4 quart pan and add, tilting bottom of pan to coat:
2 Tablespoons olive oil
1 medium onion, chopped
2 cups cabbage, shredded

Sauté the vegetables for 10 minutes, then stir in:
1 cup seitan, diced
2 cloves garlic, minced
1 (16 oz.) can tomatoes, diced
4 cups warm vegetable stock
1 teaspoon basil
1 teaspoon oregano
⅛ teaspoon black pepper

Bring soup to a bubbling simmer, stir in:
1 (16 oz.) package mixed frozen vegetables

Cover, reduce heat and cook 10 minutes until vegetables are tender.

Add:
¾ cup packaged orzo (about 4 ounces),
   or substitute 2 cups any cooked leftover pasta
1 cup hot water

Cover and simmer soup about 5 minutes, stirring occasionally.

Serve with thick crusty rolls.

Per Serving: Calories: 129, Protein: 9 gm., Carbohydrates: 20 gm., Fat: 2 gm.

MOCK CLAM CHOWDER

6 to 8 servings (about 3½ quarts)

The addition of hijiki, a sea vegetable, imparts a subtle "fresh-from -the-sea" flavor to this hearty chowder. You can find it in many Asian or natural food markets, or obtain it from one of the sources on pg. 128.

Place in a bowl:
> **1 cup instant gluten flour (vital wheat gluten)**

Combine in a measuring cup:
> **¾ cup water**
> **1 teaspoon garlic powder**
> **¼ teaspoon salt**

Mix liquid into gluten flour, kneading at the end to combine. Squeeze out into a roll about 12" long. Cut into eight pieces.

Combine in a soup pot:
> **3 cups water**
> **¼ cup hijiki, crumbled into small pieces**
> **the gluten pieces**

Bring to a boil, reduce heat and simmer for 30 minutes. Remove the cooked seitan. Set the cooking liquid aside to use later, draining first. After seitan has cooled enough to work with squeeze out excess liquid and dice small. In another pan cook until just tender:
> **4 medium potatoes, peeled and cut into ½" cubes**

When potatoes are tender drain, reserving 1 cup cooking water. In a 6 quart pan sauté until onions start to turn brown:
> **2 Tablespoons soy margarine**
> **1¼ cup onion, minced finely**

Whisk together in a small bowl until smooth:
> **¼ cup unbleached flour**
> **¼ cup soy milk**

Add to the onions and stir well. Slowly add:
> **1 cup potato cooking water**
> **½ cup hijiki broth from cooking seitan**
> **½ teaspoon salt**

As this becomes hot, stir in:
1 quart soy milk
the diced seitan
the cooked potatoes
2 Tablespoons fresh parsley, minced
black pepper to taste

When chowder is hot, ladle into bowls or mugs and serve with chowder crackers or hot biscuits.

Per Serving: Calories: 309, Protein: 30 gm., Carbohydrates: 39 gm., Fat: 5 gm.

WARM POTATO SALAD

Serves 4 to 6

This is a very easy, yet delicious, potato salad.

Cook about 15 minutes or until tender in enough boiling water to cover:

**1½ lb. red potatoes (about 6 medium),
scrubbed and cut in half**

Drain and slice the potatoes.

In a separate jar, combine until well blended:

**½ cup scallions, sliced
2 Tablespoons brown rice vinegar
2 Tablespoons prepared mustard
1 Tablespoon olive oil**

Add to the potatoes:

**8 oz. seitan, sliced diagonally in 1" squares, ½" thick (2½ cups)
the liquid ingredients**

Toss to coat the potatoes and seitan well. Garnish with cherry tomatoes, if desired, and serve warm.

Per Serving: Calories: 182, Protein: 18 gm., Carbohydrates: 25 gm., Fat: 3 gm.

LEMON RICE CASHEW SALAD
Serves 6

A "natural foods deli" type of cold salad
for a gourmet luncheon or lunch box treat.

First, toast over medium heat in a dry 2 quart pan for 5-7 minutes:
1 cup brown basmati rice

Add:

2 cups water
½ teaspoon salt

Cover the pan, bring to a boil, then reduce heat and cook about 40 minutes, until rice is tender. All of the liquid should be absorbed. When rice is cooked turn it out onto a large platter to cool.

Have ready:

2 cups ground seitan or BROWN BITS (pg. 34)
1 whole lemon for zest and juice
6 green onions, sliced ¼" thick, using part of the green tops
3 Tablespoons fresh parsley, minced

Over the rice grate the zest (the outer peel) from the lemon, being careful not to get the bitter white membrane. Squeeze the lemon for its juice into a small bowl. Stir into the lemon juice:

3 to 4 Tablespoons olive oil

In a salad bowl mix the cold rice, the seitan pieces, the onions and parsley. Then toss with the lemon and oil dressing, mixing until every piece of rice glistens. Stir in last:

½ cup roasted cashew nuts, chopped coarsely

Taste salad and add a little salt if desired.

Per Serving: Calories: 257, Protein: 22 gm., Carbohydrates: 20 gm., Fat: 13 gm.

Spinach, Mushroom and Brown Bits Salad

Serves 6 to 8

A succulent salad with crunch and protein.

Wash and pat dry:
> **2 lbs. fresh spinach**
> **4 oz. mushrooms**

Tear up the spinach leaves, discarding stems. Slice the mushrooms and have ready:
> **½ cup red onion, thinly sliced and separated into rings**
> **1 cup seitan Brown Bits**

Whiz in a blender for a dressing:
> **2 Tablespoons lemon juice**
> **1 teaspoon honey**
> **½ teaspoon Dijon mustard**
> **¼ teaspoon salt**
> **¼ cup olive oil**

In a large salad bowl, toss the spinach, mushroom and onions with the dressing until well mixed and glistening. Toss in the brown bits and serve at once.

Per Serving: Calories: 184, Protein: 17 gm., Carbohydrates: 11 gm., Fat: 10 gm.

Brown Bits

Have ready:
> **2 cups ground seitan**

Heat a large skillet and when hot, add, tilting pan to cover bottom:
> **1 Tablespoon olive oil**

Add the ground seitan to the pan, spreading it out evenly. Cook over medium high heat to lightly brown, stirring and turning to prevent burning. This will keep 2 to 3 days in the refrigerator in a covered container.

Per Tablespoon: Calories: 17, Protein: 4 gm., Carbohydrates: 1 gm., Fat: 1 gm.

PASTA PENNE WITH PEPPERS

Serves 4 to 6

This salad is great for a picnic or potluck. The peppers give it a sweet taste. Penne is a thick, cylindrical pasta, easy for children to pick up and eat. Other pastas would work well in this recipe; experiment with soy, whole wheat, spinach or corn pasta, or soba (buckwheat) noodles.

Bring to a boil in a large pot:
4 quarts water

Drop in and simmer for 30 seconds:
4 oz. snow peas, with stem ends trimmed off

Without draining off the water in the pot, remove peas with a strainer when bright green and rinse under cold water. Drain peas well and set aside.

Return water to a boil and cook to al dente:
12 oz. penne pasta

Drain, rinse in cold water, set aside.

Mix together in a large bowl
½ cup soy mayonnaise
2 Tablespoons lemon juice
1 teaspoon salt
½ teaspoon freshly ground pepper

Add and toss to coat:
8 oz. seitan, sliced ¼" thick (2 cups)
1 medium carrot, grated
½ medium red pepper, cut in thin strips
the snow peas
the cooked pasta

Serve at room temperature.

Per Serving: Calories: 333, Protein: 30 gm., Carbohydrates: 50 gm., Fat: 7 gm.

ORIENTAL PASTA SALAD
WITH PEANUT SAUCE

Serves 4

*This will provide a wonderful introduction to udon noodles,
an Oriental pasta similar in shape to linguine.*

Cook according to package directions:
> 1 (8.8 oz.) package udon noodles
> or linguine

Drain, rinse in cold water and set aside in a large bowl.

Blanch in boiling water until bright in color (about 3-5 minutes):
> 1 cup broccoli flowers and stems, cut in bite-size pieces
> 1 medium carrot, cut in matchsticks

Add to noodles and combine:
> 8 oz. seitan, cut in bite-size pieces (2 cups)
> ½ medium red pepper, cut in small strips
> ¼ cup toasted sesame seeds*
> the blanched vegetables

To make the sauce, mix in a suribachi (Japanese mortar), mortar and pestle, or in a blender:
> ¼ cup warm water
> 2 Tablespoons peanut butter
> 2 Tablespoons tamari
> 2 Tablespoons sesame or corn oil
> 1 Tablespoon brown rice vinegar
> ½ teaspoon ground ginger
> ¼ teaspoon cayenne pepper
> 2 cloves garlic, pressed

Pour over noodle-vegetable-seitan mixture and let sit overnight in the refrigerator. Serve chilled.

*Seeds can be toasted until lightly brown and aromatic, stirring in a dry skillet over medium heat or in a toaster oven. Watch carefully that they don't burn.

Per Serving: Calories: 472, Protein: 35 gm., Carbohydrates: 55 gm., Fat: 14 gm.

SUBMARINE SANDWICH

6 servings

A hearty lunch, or delicious picnic fare with each wedge wrapped separately.

Split in half lengthwise:
1 long loaf Italian or French bread

Have ready:
1 small red onion, thinly sliced
2 tomatoes, thinly sliced
1 cup seitan, thinly sliced
6 thin slices soy cheese (optional)
8 large lettuce leaves

Mix together:
2 Tablespoons eggless or soy mayonnaise
2 Tablespoons Dijon mustard

Fry until lightly browned:
1 Tablespoon olive oil
4 oz. mushrooms, thinly sliced

Spread the top half of the bread with the mustard-mayo mixture. On the bottom half spread the fried mushrooms, then put the slices of onion, tomato, seitan, cheese and lettuce on in layers. If desired, include a layer of thin slices of bread and butter pickles. Cover with the top half of bread and press loaf together. Cut into 6 large wedges and serve.

Per Serving: Calories: 240, Protein: 16 gm., Carbohydrates: 29 gm., Fat: 7 gm.

SLOPPY JOES

Serves 4

Sauté in a medium saucepan until transparent:
1 medium onion, minced
½ medium green pepper, minced
1 teaspoon sesame oil

Add and simmer 15 minutes until thoroughly heated:
8 oz. seitan, cubed or ground (2 cups)
2 cups tomato sauce

Serve on whole wheat buns with baked beans and cole slaw, or as a sauce over brown rice.

Per Serving: Calories: 117, Protein: 21 gm., Carbohydrates: 11 gm., Fat: 1.5 gm.

CRICK'S SEITAN SAUSAGE

Makes 16 to 20 patties

Grind in a blender or food processor:
8 oz. seitan (2 cups)

Combine in a mixing bowl with:
5 Tablespoons soy flour
2 Tablespoons safflower oil
2 teaspoons sage
½-1 teaspoon salt
½ teaspoon dry mustard
¼-½ teaspoon crushed red pepper

Shape into thin 2" patties. Pan fry on both sides until brown or oven bake at 400° for 15-20 minutes.

Each Patty: Calories: 41, Protein: 6 gm., Carbohydrates: 1 gm., Fat: 2 gm.

SAUSAGE PATTIES

16 patties

These are low in fat but full of flavor. If you don't have any ground seitan, you can make them right from instant gluten flour. You may want to double the recipe to have some for freezing.

Mix well in a bowl:
> **1 cup instant gluten flour (vital wheat gluten)**
> **2 teaspoons fennel seeds**
> **2 teaspoons sage**
> **1 teaspoon marjoram**
> **1 teaspoon cumin**
> **½ teaspoon dry mustard**
> **¼ teaspoon ground black pepper**

Measure into another bowl:
> **⅔ cup warm water**
> **1 Tablespoon tamari**
> **1 Tablespoon maple syrup**
> **1 Tablespoon olive oil**

Add liquid ingredients to gluten flour and spices, adding a little more water if needed. Knead into a smooth ball, and divide and stretch into 16 patties. For the cooking stock combine in a kettle:
> **3 cups water**
> **2 Tablespoons tamari**

Put patties into stock, cover and bring to a boil. Reduce heat and gently simmer for 50 minutes. Either serve warm as is, or dip patties into flour and quickly pan fry in a little bit of oil to brown and crisp the outside. For a crisper texture, cook patties by baking first, then simmering. Place the patties on a lightly oiled baking sheet and bake in a 350° oven for 20 minutes. They will puff up and be crusty. Prick patties with a fork and drop the puffs into the simmering stock and cook for 30 minutes.

Per Serving: Calories: 38, Protein: 7 gm., Carbohydrates: 2 gm., Fat: 1 gm.

SAUSAGE GRAVY AND BISCUITS

Makes 2 cups

A breakfast treat that takes very little time to make.

Heat a large skillet and add, tilting pan to coat with oil:
1 to 2 Tablespoons olive oil
1 cup ground seitan

Cook over medium high heat 5 to 10 minutes until lightly browned. Sprinkle seitan with:
1 Tablespoon flour
1 teaspoon sage
½ teaspoon salt
¼ teaspoon black pepper

Mix well, then stir in:
1 cup cold soymilk

Mixture will bubble up and thicken. Stir in:
1 cup warm vegetable stock

Cook a minute or two more. When it bubbles ladle onto:
8 hot biscuits, split in half

Per Serving (includes 1 biscuit): Calories: 97, Protein: 7 gm., Carbohydrates: 14 gm., Fat: 4 gm.

Barbecued "Rinds"

8 servings

Crunchy, chewy "rinds" or "ribs" are made with gluten that puffs up and crisps in the oven. These are treats for a picnic or lunch box.

Lightly oil 2 baking sheets and preheat oven to 350°.

Mix together with a whisk or fork:
 1 cup instant gluten flour (vital wheat gluten)
 1 Tablespoon nutritional yeast

Measure into a bowl:
 1⅛ cup warm water

Stir the water into the gluten flour. The resulting gluten should be quite wet. Roll and stretch it out as flat as possible. Cut into 24 strips about ½" wide and 6" long, placing strips on baking sheets. Bake 15 to 20 minutes. Strips will puff up and turn golden. Remove pans from oven and prick each "rib" with a fork in several places. Turn over and pour on evenly:
 1 cup barbecue sauce

Return baking sheets to oven and cook 10 to15 minutes more. Serve ribs hot or move to a rack to cool.

Per Serving: Calories: 79, Protein: 15 gm., Carbohydrates: 7 gm., Fat: 1 gm.

BARBECUE SLICES

6 servings

These can be served immediately in buns or stored in the freezer for later use.

Stir together in one bowl:
> **1 cup instant gluten flour (vital wheat gluten)**
> **1 Tablespoon nutritional yeast**

Measure into a cup:
> **⅔ cup warm water**
> **2 Tablespoons catsup**
> **1 Tablespoon olive oil**

Mix wet and dry ingredients together well, shape into a thick roll and cook in a stock of:
> **3 cups water**
> **1 Tablespoon tamari**

Simmer for about 50 minutes, then let cool in the stock for 10 minutes. Remove roll and slice into 24 or more thin slices, cutting on the diagonal to get wider pieces.

Heat in a 2 quart pan:
> **2 cups barbecue sauce**

Add the sliced seitan and simmer a few minutes. If seitan has been made ahead and chilled, heat in the barbecue sauce until hot. Serve with crusty rolls and potato salad.

Per Serving: Calories: 164, Protein: 21 gm., Carbohydrates: 16 gm., Fat: 4 gm.

CORNMEAL CUTLETS

Serves 4

Slice into ¼" thick pieces: (8–5"x 2" slices)
8 oz. seitan

Dust pieces on each side to cover in:
¾ cup cornmeal

Heat a medium frying pan and add:
1 Tablespoon corn oil

When oil is hot, add dusted seitan pieces and fry over low heat on each side until golden brown (about 5 minutes per side.) Serve with mushroom gravy, or a side dish of rice or potatoes, and a green salad.

Per Serving: Calories: 180, Protein: 21 gm., Carbohydrates: 20 gm., Fat: 5 gm.

GOLDEN BAKED BEANS

Serves 4

These beans are not really baked, although they taste like it. As few of us heat our homes with the cookstove these days, I find it more economical to simmer them on top of the stove. Leftover beans are great for picnics. The seitan in this recipe replaces the traditional pork.

Soak at least 8 hours or overnight in enough water to cover:
> **2 cups navy beans (or other beans of your choice)**
> **1 (5") strip kombu (optional)**

An alternative method to soaking the beans is parboiling them for 15 minutes, removing from heat and letting them sit for 1 hour. Rinse beans, drain and cook with the following for 1 hour or until beans are somewhat tender:
> **6 cups fresh water**
> **1 medium onion, chopped**

If using kombu, remove, cut in squares and return to the pot. Skim off any foam that develops while cooking.

At the end of the hour, add:
> **8 oz. seitan, cut in small cubes (2 cups)**
> **1 cup vegetable stock**
> **¼ cup molasses or other sweetener**
> **2 Tablespoons prepared mustard**
> **2 Tablespoons miso**
> **2 Tablespoons tamari**
> **⅛ teaspoon cinnamon**

Simmer for at least 20 minutes or until desired consistency is reached.

Per Serving: Calories: 354, Protein: 37 gm., Carbohydrates: 75 gm., Fat: 2 gm.

ALL - AMERICAN POT PIE

6 servings

This recipe is a real winner.
For children, make small individual pies in separate tiny pans or ceramic bowls.

For filling, have ready:
1 recipe SHEPHERD'S PIE (pg. 80)

Preheat oven to 375°.

For the crust combine:
2 cups whole wheat pastry flour
1 cup unbleached white flour
½ teaspoon salt

Add all at once:
½ cup corn oil

Work oil into the flour with a fork until flour is in pea-size balls.

Make a well in the flour mixture and add all at once:
½ cup cold water

Stir with a fork only enough to moisten and until flour holds together. You may have to add a bit more water to make that happen. If so, add slowly by the tablespoonful.

Divide dough in half and roll out between two sheets of waxed paper or on a well-floured board. Place pie crust in a 9" pie pan. Fill with the **SHEPHERD'S PIE** recipe. Place other pie crust on top and fold under the edges to seal. Finish edge of crust using your favorite method. (Pinching between the fingers or pressing with the tines of a fork are both effective.) Make small slits in the top crust in 8 places. Bake for 50 minutes.

Per Serving: Calories: 505, Protein: 23 gm., Carbohydrates: 76 gm., Fat: 22 gm.

HERBED GROUND SEITAN LOAF

18 to 20 slices

A "down home" favorite with marvelous taste and texture. Leftover loaf makes excellent "luncheon-meat type" sandwiches.

Grind in a food processor or grinder:
12 oz. seitan (3 cups)

Sauté in a hot skillet:
2 Tablespoons olive oil
1 medium onion, finely chopped

Measure into a large bowl:
2 cups cracker or bread crumbs
2 Tablespoons parsley, minced
2 Tablespoons catsup
1 teaspoon thyme
1 teaspoon oregano
1 teaspoon basil
½ teaspoon salt
⅛ teaspoon black pepper

Add the cooked onions to the seasoned crumbs, then mix with the ground seitan. For a finely textured loaf return all ingredients to the processor and blend. Preheat oven to 350°. Lightly oil a loaf pan and pack the seitan ingredients down. Bake loaf 30 minutes, lay a piece of foil over top of pan and cook 30 minutes more. Let cool for 10 minutes before slicing.

Per Slice: Calories: 85, Protein: 8 gm., Carbohydrates: 10 gm., Fat: 2 gm.

BRAISED SEITAN WITH ONIONS

6 to 8 servings

A *satisfying home-style recipe for fried onion lovers.*

Mix in a 2-quart bowl:
> **1 cup instant gluten flour (vital wheat gluten)**
> **1 Tablespoon nutritional yeast**
> **1 teaspoon cumin**
> **½ teaspoon marjoram**

Combine in a measuring cup:
> **¾ cup water**
> **1 Tablespoon tamari**

Stir the liquid and dry ingredients together, kneading the mixture at the end to combine thoroughly. Shape into 16 flat patties or medallions.

Bring to a boil in a 4 quart sauce pan:
> **2 cups vegetable stock**
> **1 Tablespoon tamari**

Add patties, cover and simmer about 50 minutes. While the patties are simmering, heat a large skillet and add:
> **2 Tablespoons olive oil**
> **3 large onions, sliced thinly**

Sauté the onions over low heat, stirring occasionally so they cook evenly and do not burn, 30 to 40 minutes. Onions will turn a golden brown. Drain the patties, dip lightly into flour and fry in a lightly oiled pan a few minutes on each side to brown. Place patties on a platter and top with the fried onions.

Per Serving: Calories: 137, Protein: 20 gm., Carbohydrates: 9 gm., Fat: 5 gm.

OVEN ROASTED NUGGETS

16 pieces

Great finger food that kids will enjoy eating hot or cold.

Stir together completely:
    1 cup instant gluten flour (vital wheat gluten)
    1 Tablespoon nutritional yeast
    1 teaspoon marjoram
    1 teaspoon onion powder
    ½ teaspoon sage
    ½ teaspoon salt

In another bowl measure:
    ¾ cup warm water
    1 Tablespoon tamari
    1 Tablespoon olive oil

Mix wet and dry ingredients together, stirring quickly. Squeeze out any excess liquid and divide into 16 pieces. Stretch and flatten each piece into a small cutlet and drop into a pot that has simmering:
    2 cups vegetable stock

Cover pot and simmer for 45 minutes.

To prepare breading mixture, combine in a medium bowl:
    2 cups finely crushed cracker crumbs*
    1 Tablespoon nutritional yeast
    ½ teaspoon paprika
    ½ teaspoon thyme
    ¼ teaspoon black pepper

Preheat oven to 350°. Drain the pieces of seitan, pressing to remove excess liquid. Pat each piece in the breading mixture. Place the breaded nuggets on a lightly oiled baking sheet. Bake nuggets 10 to 15 minutes, turn over and bake 10 minutes more until a light golden brown. Don't overbake or they will be too chewy.

For a delicious variation on the breading substitute ½ cup toasted slivered almonds for ½ cup of the cracker crumbs.

Per Nugget: Calories: 84, Protein: 9 gm., Carbohydrates: 11 gm., Fat: 2 gm.

Root Vegetable Stew

Serves 4-6

*Ingredients for this stew can vary according to what's in season.
You can add leftover beans or grains, tofu, or change the spices to suit your
taste. Squash and cabbage can be used as the main vegetables;
sea vegetables such as kombu and wakame add a nice touch.
Green peas or fresh corn make a delightful summer stew.*

Sauté in a medium sauce pan in the order given over low heat for 10 minutes:

1 Tablespoon sesame oil
2 medium onions, chopped coarsely
2 carrots, cut in ¼" rounds
2 parsnips, cut in ¼" rounds
2 turnips, cut in 1" cubes

Add:

8 oz. seitan, cut in ½" cubes (2½ cups)
vegetable stock to cover vegetables halfway (approx. 1 cup)
1 teaspoon basil

Cover pan and simmer for 20 minutes (or until vegetables are tender).

Add and stir constantly until thickened:

1-2 Tablespoons arrowroot, diluted in 4 Tablespoons water

Serve with brown rice and a green salad or cooked leafy greens.

Per Serving: Calories: 182, Protein: 18 gm., Carbohydrates: 26 gm., Fat: 3 gm.

CREOLE GUMBO

6 servings

Browning the flour is the flavor secret of this Cajun favorite.

Heat a large cast iron skillet and sprinkle evenly with:
¼ cup unbleached flour

Cook the flour over medium heat until golden brown, stirring frequently with a spatula and watching carefully so it doesn't burn. Set it aside to cool; pan will be hot after removing from stove, so continue to stir for a minute.

In a separate pan, cook 5 minutes (or microwave for 2 minutes) until softened:
1 Tablespoon olive oil
2 cloves garlic, minced
1 large onion, chopped
1 green pepper, diced
1 rib celery, diced small

In a 4 quart sauce pan add the softened vegetables to:
1 (28 oz.) can tomatoes, cut up
2 cups vegetable stock
1 (10 oz.) package frozen okra
8 oz. seitan, diced in ½" cubes (2½ cups)
½ teaspoon oregano
½ teaspoon thyme
¼ teaspoon black pepper
⅛ teaspoon cayenne

Bring to a boil, then reduce heat, cover pan and simmer on low heat 10 minutes. Check to be sure okra is cooked. Pour 2-3 Tablespoons of the hot liquid from the gumbo into the browned flour, stir and let cool. Add a cup more of the hot liquid and then stir the mixture into the gumbo to thicken it. Taste and add a little Tabasco or hot sauce if desired. The gumbo will be like a thick stew. Serve on hot cooked rice.

Per Serving: Calories: 136, Protein: 16 gm., Carbohydrates: 17 gm., Fat: 3 gm.

TURKEY ROLL WITH STUFFING

Serves 12 to 16

Miyoko Nishimoto created this spectacular dish for her Now and Zen Epicure cookbook. My recipe is a little different and equally dazzling when served on your best holiday platter. The crisp brown skin is made of yuba, the skin that forms on hot soy milk. Yuba is dried and sold packaged in Asian markets. If desired, you can cook the gluten several days in advance of the feast and keep the roll refrigerated. It can also be prepared weeks ahead and frozen until needed. Wrap well in several layers of plastic wrap to store. Bring to room temperature before stuffing. An attractive accompaniment on your "turkey" platter is hollowed-out orange halves with whole berry cranberry sauce filling.

Prepare a seasoning mixture by combining in a blender or food processor:

½ cup nutritional yeast flakes   **1 teaspoon sage**
  (See page 18)
1 teaspoon marjoram   **1 teaspoon salt**
1 teaspoon thyme

Reserve 1 Tablespoon of the seasoning mix to add to the gravy later.

Transfer seasoning to a large bowl and mix in, one cup at a time:
6 cups instant gluten flour (vital wheat gluten)

Measure into a bowl:
4½ cups warm water
2 Tablespoons tamari
2 Tablespoons safflower oil

Mix the liquid and dry ingredients, adding more water if needed for firm but moist gluten. Roll out, pull and stretch the gluten into a rectangle approximately 8" x 16". Brush the surface lightly with a mild olive oil.

Cut 1 yard of cheesecloth (double in thickness), rinse in water, squeeze out and lay flat on your work surface. Place gluten on cheesecloth; fold sides of the cloth over gluten and roll up the short side. If you cover the gluten with this cheesecloth "skin," the roll won't stick to itself while cooking and be hard to unroll later. Don't roll too tightly; you need some room for the gluten to expand as it absorbs liquid. Tie a string around the roll and place it in a very large pot. The roll will be good-sized, so be sure to use a pot big enough to hold it, as well as some simmering liquid.

Add to the pot:

4 quarts of hot water	**½ cup onion slices**
some celery leaves	**¼ teaspoon peppercorns**
1 bay leaf	

Add the gluten roll, cover the pot and simmer for about one and one half hours, turning it over once or twice. It's important that all parts of the roll cook *under* the stock for at least an hour. Let the roll cool in the stock.

To assemble have ready:
3-4 sheets yuba (approx. 1 oz.)
2 quarts water for soaking

Let the yuba soak for 5 to 10 minutes, handling it gently. The dark, dry bean curd sheets will turn light in color and become pliable for wrapping the roll. Unroll the seitan from the cheesecloth, stretching it as flat as you can. Spread with the stuffing mixture. Roll up like a jelly roll, starting with the shortest end. Have a large oiled baking pan ready. Place the stuffed roll in the baking pan, stuffed side down, and wrap the wet yuba sheets around the roll, completely enclosing it.

Mix together for basting:
¼ cup safflower oil
2 Tablespoons tamari

Preheat oven to 350°. Baste roast with oil mixture, place in oven and roast for 1½ hours, basting every 20 minutes. If roast begins to get too brown, cover with aluminum foil.

To prepare stuffing, sauté 10 minutes until soft:
2 Tablespoons safflower oil
1 medium onion, chopped small
1 cup celery, chopped small

Add to softened onions and celery:

¼ cup parsley, minced	**½ teaspoon salt**
1 teaspoon thyme	**¼ teaspoon black pepper**
1 teaspoon sage	**¾ cup vegetable stock**

Have ready in a large bowl:
    8 cups dry bread pieces, torn up

Mix the dry bread with the onions and stock, adding a little more liquid if needed to moisten. Stuffing can be varied by substituting leftover corn bread for part of the bread pieces, adding a cup of mushrooms to the onions while sautéing or adding a tart chopped apple. If there is more stuffing than fits easily into the roll, bake the extra in a separate dish along with the roast for 30 to 40 minutes.

When the roast is cooked, lift it out carefully onto a large platter and carve as you would a large rolled roast. Any drippings in the pan can be used in the gravy.

Per Serving Without Gravy: Calories: 594, Protein: 79 gm., Carbohydrates: 74 gm., Fat: 15 gm.

To make the gravy, combine in a sauce pan (or 2-quart measure if using a microwave):
    2 Tablespoons soy margarine
    ¼ cup flour
    1 Tablespoon seasoning mix
        (reserved from beginning of recipe)
    1 Tablespoon nutritional yeast flakes

Cook a minute or two, then whisk in:
    any pan drippings
    3 cups vegetable stock
    2 teaspoons tamari

Cook, stirring occasionally, until thickened and bubbly. Taste and add salt and pepper if desired.

Per Serving: Calories: 34, Protein: 1 gm., Carbohydrates: 5 gm., Fat: 1 gm.

HAWAIIAN STIR FRY
WITH PINEAPPLE

6 servings

Mix in a bowl for a marinade:
 ¼ cup tamari
 1 Tablespoon arrowroot
 2 teaspoons minced gingerroot

Stir in and let stand
 2 cups seitan, cut in thin strips 2" long

Have ready:
 2 cups cabbage, shredded
 1 medium onion, sliced thinly
 1 medium green pepper, diced
 1 rib celery, thinly sliced on diagonal

Drain, reserving the liquid for sauce:
 1 (8 oz). can pineapple tidbits

Drain the seitan strips, adding the pineapple juice to the marinade with:
 1 cup vegetable stock

Heat a large skillet or wok and add:
 1 Tablespoon sesame oil

Stir fry the seitan strips in the hot pan for 5 minutes and remove to a serving bowl. Add to the pan:
 2 teaspoons canola oil
 1 teaspoon toasted sesame oil

In the hot oil, stir fry the onion, green pepper, cabbage and celery for 5 to 10 minutes, until crisp-tender. Stir in the pineapple and seitan. Mix the marinade, juice and stock, and pour it over seitan and vegetables, stirring as it bubbles up. Pour into serving bowl and accompany with cooked brown rice or fried Chinese noodles.

Per Serving: Calories: 154, Protein: 21 gm., Carbohydrates: 13 gm., Fat: 5 gm.

ASIAN FRIED RICE

6 servings

A marvelous use for leftover seitan loaf or roll.

Have ready:
   2 cloves garlic, minced
   1 inch gingerroot, minced
   2 cups cabbage, shredded
   1 medium onion, thinly sliced
   1 carrot, thinly sliced and cut in half moons
   1 cup celery, thinly sliced on diagonal

Heat a wok or large skillet over medium high heat and add, tilting pan to coat bottom:
   1 Tablespoon sesame oil

Stir in the vegetables one at a time and stir-fry for a few minutes.

Push vegetables to one side of the pan and put in:
   2 cups cooked brown rice
      (with any clumps separated into individual grains)
   1 cup seitan BROWN BITS, pg. 34

Stir the rice and seitan to heat, then mix with the vegetables. Cover the pan and cook 1 minute. Mix in a small bowl:
   1 Tablespoon miso
   2 Tablespoons water

Stir the miso mixture into the fried rice, taste and add a little tamari if desired. Turn out into a bowl and sprinkle with:
   2 green onions, thinly sliced

Per Serving: Calories: 133, Protein: 7 gm., Carbohydrates: 19 gm., Fat: 4 gm.

BROCCOLI IN SPICY BROWN SAUCE WITH MUSHROOMS

6 servings

See photo on the cover.
The secret of the peppery hot flavor is chili oil, often used in Asian cooking.

Mix together and let stand:
2 cups seitan strips, thinly sliced
2 Tablespoons tamari

Pour 1 cup hot water over:
4 dried shiitake mushroom caps (discard stems)

Let soak 20 minutes, then carefully pour off liquid into a measuring cup, leaving any sand in the dish. Cut mushrooms into strips.

Have ready:
5 to 6 cups broccoli flowerets, blanched for 1 minute
4 large garlic cloves, pressed
1 large onion, thinly sliced

To the mushroom soaking liquid add enough vegetable stock to make 2 cups, then stir in and set aside:
1 Tablespoon tamari   1 Tablespoon arrowroot

Heat a large frying pan or wok and add, tilting to coat bottom of pan:
1 Tablespoon chili oil, pg. 57

Add the seitan strips and stir fry over medium high heat for a few minutes, then remove to a serving dish. Heat the pan again, tilting to add:
1 Tablespoon chili oil

Quickly stir fry the garlic, onion slices and mushrooms for 3-4 minutes. Add the broccoli. Cook 1 minute, return seitan to pan and mix in. Push vegetables to one side of pan and pour in the stock with arrowroot. It will begin to thicken almost immediately; stir with all the vegetables. Add:
4 green onions, thinly sliced
1 Tablespoon toasted sesame seeds (optional)

Pour onto the serving platter. Serve with brown rice.

Per Serving: Calories: 131, Protein: 15 gm., Carbohydrates: 12 gm., Fat: 5 gm.

CHILI OIL

Makes ½ cup

A few drops of this will add zing to any dish.

Mix in a blender or processor:
2 Tablespoons dried red chili pepper flakes
½ cup safflower oil

Simmer in a small saucepan, covered, for 6-7 minutes, or place in a one-quart measuring cup or serving dish, cover with plastic wrap and microwave on full power for 3 minutes; pierce plastic and let cool. Pour into a clean bottle and store on a cool pantry shelf. It will keep indefinitely.

To use, tip bottle and pour out oil slowly, leaving pepper flakes on the side of the bottle.

Per Tablespoon: Calories: 119, Protein: 0, Carbohydrates: 0, Fat: 14 gm.

Vegetarian Egg Rolls

Serves 4 to 6 (about 20 medium egg rolls)

Everybody loves egg rolls, and they are fun to make at home. The trick to egg rolls is to drain and completely cool the filling before rolling them. Make sure to buy egg roll wrappers that contain no dye.

Sauté in a wok or cast iron skillet until transparent:
   1 medium onion, minced
   1 Tablespoon sesame or safflower oil

Add and simmer until cabbage is tender, covering if necessary:
   ½ medium cabbage, shredded
   1 medium carrot, grated

Add to cabbage, then set aside to cool:
   2 cups mung bean sprouts
   8 oz. seitan, chopped finely or ground (2 cups)
   tamari to taste

Have ready:
   1 (16 oz.) package egg roll wrappers

To fill the egg rolls, take one wrapper and place on a flat surface with one corner toward you. Take about ⅓ cup of the filling and place it across that corner, shaping the filling into a 1" long cylinder. Lift the corner over the filling and begin to roll, tucking the point of the wrapper under the filling. Roll into a cylinder about 4" long, until wrapper just covers the filling. Brush the remaining edges of the wrapper with water. Bring the two side corners up over the top of the enclosed filling and gently press down. Continue rolling filling over the remaining wrapper edge. The water will seal the edges and keep the wrapper intact. Cover with a kitchen towel until ready to cook. You can either bake or fry the egg rolls.

To fry, heat in a wok or heavy pan:
   1 cup peanut or corn oil

When the oil is hot, add the egg rolls and cook until crispy. Turn and cook until the other side is crispy. Drain on paper towels. The remaining oil can be saved and used for future egg rolls or tempura as long as it hasn't gotten smoky while frying. Cover and store in a cool place, adding an umeboshi plum to keep it fresh, if desired.

To bake egg rolls, preheat oven to 400°, place rolls in a baking pan and brush lightly with oil. Bake 15 minutes, turn rolls over with tongs and bake 10 minutes more until slightly crispy on the outside. This method uses much less oil and is equally delicious.

Per Serving: Calories: 271, Protein: 21 gm., Carbohydrates: 36 gm., Fat: 7 gm.

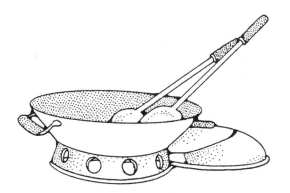

HOISEN SEITAN

Serves 4

Mix together in a medium sauce pan:
>   1½ cups apple-peach juice or plain apple juice
>   3 Tablespoons miso, dissolved in 2 Tablespoons water
>   2 Tablespoons barley malt or other sweetener
>   1 Tablespoon brown rice vinegar
>   1 Tablespoon arrowroot,
>   dissolved in 2 Tablespoons apple juice or water
>   1 teaspoon ground ginger

Cook over medium heat, stirring constantly until arrowroot thickens slightly.

Preheat oven to 350°. Place in a 2 quart glass or ceramic baking dish:
>   8 oz. seitan, cut in strips or cubes (2 cups)

Pour sauce over seitan and bake for 20 minutes. If desired, place green pepper and tomato slices on top before baking for a more colorful dish. For a quicker dish, make sauce and add seitan until thoroughly heated, about 5 minutes. Serve over hot brown rice.

Per Serving: Calories: 183, Protein: 20 gm., Carbohydrates: 31 gm., Fat: 1 gm.

Chow Mein

6 servings

If vegetables are prepared ahead this can be cooked in short order.

Have ready:
   2 cups seitan, cut in ½" cubes
   1 medium onion, diced
   2 carrots, thinly sliced
   2 cups napa or Chinese cabbage, shredded
   3 ribs celery, thinly sliced

Combine in a bowl and set aside:
   2 cups vegetable stock
   2 Tablespoons arrowroot
   1 Tablespoon tamari
   1 teaspoon powdered ginger
   ¼ teaspoon garlic powder

Heat a skillet or wok and add:
   1 Tablespoon sesame oil

Stir fry diced onion in the hot oil 2 minutes over medium high heat. Add cabbage, carrots and celery, stir fry 2 minutes, reduce heat and cover pan. Cook 2 minutes, remove cover, stir and push vegetables to one side. Add to the empty side of pan:
   1 Tablespoon sesame oil

Stir fry cubes of seitan until hot. Mix with vegetables. Stir liquids and arrowroot, pour into pan and mix well. When sauce begins to bubble remove from heat and serve over brown rice or chow mein noodles.

Per Serving: Calories: 135, Protein: 21 gm., Carbohydrates: 13 gm., Fat: 3 gm.

Chinese Balls in Sweet Sour Sauce

makes 16 balls

This dish takes some time to prepare but is a real treat.

Measure into a 2 quart bowl:
> **3 cups ground seitan**
> **½ cup green pepper, diced in ¼" pieces**
> **6 green onions, sliced in ¼" pieces**
> **1 (8 oz.) can water chestnuts, drained and chopped small**
> **2 Tablespoons parsley, minced**

Mix in a small bowl:
> **1 Tablespoon tahini**
> **2 Tablespoons tamari**
> **1 teaspoon gingerroot, minced or grated**

Stir the tahini mixture into the seitan and vegetables. When well mixed, stir in:
> **⅔ cup unbleached or whole wheat flour**

On a wide plate or platter spread a mixture of:
> **½ cup unbleached flour**
> **1 teaspoon paprika**

Shape about ¼ cup of the seitan mixture into a ball and gently roll in the seasoned flour. Repeat until all the mixture has been used. Ground seitan will vary in moisture content. If it's too moist and balls are not holding together add a little more flour to the mixture. Heat a large skillet over medium high heat and add, tipping pan so bottom is well coated:
> **1 Tablespoon safflower oil**
> **1 teaspoon toasted sesame oil**

Place each ball gently into the skillet, being careful not to crowd the pan. Turn each carefully as it browns. When the last ball is lightly browned, reduce heat to very low, cover the pan tightly and let balls cook for 30 minutes, turning once to make sure they are cooking evenly.

To prepare the sweet and sour sauce, boil for 2 minutes in a small covered saucepan:

1 large carrot, very thinly sliced
1 cup water

Strain the stock, saving carrot slices to add last. Stir into the liquid:

¼ cup honey
⅓ cup cider vinegar

Dissolve in a small bowl, then add to sauce and stir until thickened:

1 Tablespoon arrowroot
¼ cup cold water

Arrange balls on a serving plate. Add carrot slices to sauce and pour sauce into a dish to pass with the balls.

Per Ball: Calories: 92, Protein: 9 gm., Carbohydrates: 14 gm., Fat: 2 gm.

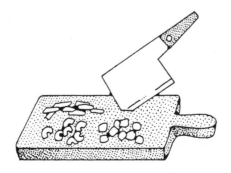

ROASTED ALMONDS AND DICED SEITAN

6 servings

Almonds add crunch and flavor in this recipe.

Mix for a marinade:
> **1 Tablespoon arrowroot**
> **2 Tablespoons tamari**
> **1 cup vegetable stock**

Stir in and let marinate while preparing vegetables:
> **2 cups seitan, cut in ½" cubes**

Have ready:
> **1 medium onion, chopped**
> **1 cup carrots, thinly sliced**
> **1 cup celery, thinly sliced on the diagonal**
> **1 cup green snow peas, strings removed and cut in half**
> **2 cups mung or lentil bean sprouts, rinsed**

Heat a wok or large skillet, and when hot add:
> **1 Tablespoon sesame oil**

Remove seitan from marinade, reserving liquid. Toss diced seitan into hot pan, stir fry a few minutes and remove. To hot pan, add:
> **1 Tablespoon sesame oil**

Add onion, carrots, celery and cook 5 minutes, stirring from time to time. Add the snow peas and bean sprouts, cook 2 minutes more, then return the seitan to pan. Pour the leftover marinade over the vegetables. Stir in last:
> **½ cup roasted almonds, sliced**

Serve over brown rice.

Per Serving: Calories: 230, Protein: 24 gm., Carbohydrates: 16 gm,. Fat: 11 gm.

SWEET STIR FRY

Serves 4

You can vary the vegetables used to make a stir fry. Try using onions, mushrooms or broccoli, sautéing the firmer vegetables first.

Heat in a wok or frying pan over medium heat:
2 Tablespoons toasted sesame oil

Sauté for 30 seconds:
1 clove garlic, minced
2 teaspoons fresh ginger, grated

Turn heat to high and add, stirring continuously for 5-8 minutes:
½ medium head cauliflower, cut in 2" flowers
3 medium carrots, sliced in ½" diagonals
½ cup fresh or frozen green beans, cut in 1" pieces

Add and bring to a boil:
8 oz. seitan, cut in very thin strips (2 cups)
½ cup mirin (rice wine)
  or water
½ teaspoon salt
½ cup vegetable stock

Lower heat and add:
2 teaspoons arrowroot dissolved in 2 Tablespoons water

Simmer about 1-2 minutes, stirring constantly. Season with tamari to taste, if you desire. Serve immediately over brown rice.

Per Serving: Calories: 193, Protein: 22 gm., Carbohydrates: 17 gm., Fat: 7 gm.

LO MEIN
OR SEITAN NOODLES
6 to 8 servings

A hearty dish for hungry people made with the fresh Chinese noodles that can be found in the produce section of a supermarket.

Mix well for a marinade:

1 cup vegetable stock	2 Tablespoons tamari
1 Tablespoon arrowroot	1 teaspoon CHILI OIL, pg. 57
1 teaspoon honey	

Stir into the marinade:
2 cups seitan, sliced in thin strips

Have ready:

1 cup celery, diced	1 red bell pepper, diced
1 green pepper, diced	2 oz. mushrooms, sliced

2 cups bok choy, chopped or Chinese cabbage
1 large onion, cut in thin half moons
4 green onions, cut in ¼" slices
1 (8 oz.) can water chestnuts, sliced, drained

Heat a large kettle of boiling, salted water and add:
1 (14 oz.) package of fresh Chinese noodles

Cook only 3-4 minutes; noodles should be tender but firm. Drain and set aside but keep warm. Drain the seitan, reserving marinade.

Heat a wok or large skillet and add:
1 Tablespoon toasted sesame oil

Quickly stir fry the drained seitan slices, then remove to a warm dish. Add to pan:
1 Tablespoon toasted sesame oil

Stir fry onion and pepper 2 minutes. Add cabbage, mushrooms and green onions, cook a few minutes, then add water chestnuts. Push vegetables to one side, add the marinade, and cook until it thickens. Stir in the seitan and mix with the vegetables. Use a large fork and spoon to toss the noodles and vegetables in a large bowl and serve at once.

Per Serving: Calories: 262, Protein: 24 gm., Carbohydrates: 34 gm., Fat: 6 gm.

CHOP SUEY

6 servings

This recipe is more American than Chinese, but it's quick and easy with a definite Asian touch your family will enjoy.

Marinate together in a medium bowl:
> **2 cups seitan, cut in ½" cubes**
> **1 cup vegetable stock**
> **2 Tablespoons tamari**
> **2 Tablespoons mirin or sherry (optional)**

Have ready:
> **1 medium onion, diced small**
> **1 cup mushrooms, sliced**
> **2 ribs celery, thinly sliced on diagonal**

Heat a large skillet and add:
> **1 Tablespoon sesame oil**

Stir fry the vegetables for 3 minutes. Add:
> **1 (16 oz.) can chop suey vegetables**
> **1 (8 oz.) can sliced water chestnuts, drained**

Cover the pan and simmer 2 minutes. Add the marinated seitan with liquid and stir gently as it heats, simmering a minute more. Serve immediately over crisp Chinese noodles.

Per Serving: Calories: 130, Protein: 22 gm., Carbohydrates: 11 gm., Fat: 3 gm.

Pot Stickers

Makes 40 to 42

These are Chinese dumplings, partly pan grilled, partly steamed, with a zesty filling. Kids love them and can help to make the bundles. Look for won ton wrappers in the produce department of your supermarket. As an alternative you can buy egg roll wrappers and cut them into 4 quarters to make won ton squares.

For the filling, have ready:
> **6 oz. seitan, diced small (1½ cups)**
> **2 cups cabbage, shredded and cut finely**
> **½ cup celery, diced finely**
> **½ cup green onions, chopped**
> **1 cup bean sprouts (2 ounces), chopped small**
> **2 cups mushrooms, chopped small**

Mix for a marinade:
> **2 Tablespoons tamari**
> **2 teaspoons arrowroot**
> **1 teaspoon CHILI OIL, pg. 57**
> **1 teaspoon barley malt**
> **½ teaspoon ginger powder**
> **½ teaspoon garlic powder**

Stir the diced seitan into the marinade and set aside. Heat a skillet and when hot, add and tilt pan so oil covers bottom:
> **2 teaspoons safflower oil**
> **the chopped mushrooms**

Cook a few minutes to lightly brown, then remove mushrooms to a dish.

Heat pan again and add:
> **1 teaspoon safflower oil**
> **1 teaspoon dark sesame oil**

Tilt pan so oil covers the bottom, then add the cabbage, celery and onions one at a time, cooking a few minutes until crisp-tender. Add the marinated seitan to pan, cooking a minute or two, then mix in the bean sprouts and mushrooms. Set filling aside; you will have about 3 cups.

Make a paste of:
    1 teaspoon flour
    1 teaspoon water

Keep the won ton wrappers covered with a cloth to prevent them from drying out. Put a rounded teaspoon of filling in the center of each wrapper, gather up the ends to form a bundle, using a dab of paste and pressing edges to seal. Each won ton package will have about 42 squares of the noodle dough. You can cook them in two pans or make two batches. Heat a 10" skillet and add:
    2 teaspoons safflower oil
    1 teaspoon dark sesame oil

Tilt pan so oil covers bottom, place half the bundles in the pan in a single layer and cook over medium high heat about 2 minutes. Bottoms of the pot stickers should be brown. Watch out for steam as you pour on:
    1 cup warm water

Cover the pan, reduce heat to very low and let dumplings steam for about 20 minutes. Most of the liquid will be absorbed. Remove dumplings and keep them warm as you cook the second batch. Serve with hot Chinese mustard or a dipping sauce of:
    ¼ cup tamari
    ¼ cup rice vinegar
    1 Tablespoon shredded ginger root

Each: Calories: 31, Protein: 2 gm., Carbohydrates: 3 gm., Fat:. 1 gm.

Miso Ginger Cutlets

6 to 8 servings

Sparkling with flavor, these are good hot or cold.

Stir together in a two-quart bowl:
> **1 cup instant gluten flour (vital wheat gluten)**
> **¼ teaspoon garlic powder**

Mix in a measuring cup:
> **¾ cup warm water**
> **1 Tablespoon tamari**
> **1 Tablespoon safflower oil**

Add the liquid ingredients to the instant gluten flour and knead together.

Place in a large kettle and bring to a simmer:
> **1 (6") strip kombu**
> **4 cups water**
> **2 Tablespoons tamari**

Tear the gluten mixture into 20-24 pieces, stretching each piece out into a flat round cutlet shape. Place cutlets in the cooking liquid, cover and simmer about 50 minutes.

Mix for the marinade:
> **½ cup light miso**
> **⅓ cup mirin, white wine or apple cider**
> **1" piece raw gingerroot, grated or minced**

When cutlets are cooked, drain them and place in the marinade, turning each one to coat evenly. Let stand for an hour or overnight. Before serving, cover with plastic wrap and heat in a microwave oven for 10 minutes, or cover with foil and bake in a 350° oven 30 minutes until cutlets are piping hot.

Per Serving: Calories: 150, Protein: 16 gm., Carbohydrates: 21 gm., Fat: 3 gm.

SUKIYAKI

Serves 4

You can use any combination of vegetables in this sukiyaki, such as shiitake mushrooms, onions, carrots or burdock. Add mochi (brown rice cakes) on top at the end of cooking for a "melted" effect, if desired.

Cut in squares and place in a heavy skillet:
   2 (6") kombu strips, soaked for 10 minutes and drained

Arrange in a skillet so that each vegetable has its own corner of the pan, not layered or mixed in with the other vegetables:
   2 ribs celery, cut on large diagonals
   1 medium daikon radish
      or 1 medium turnip, cut in large chunks
   1 small butternut squash, peeled and cut in large chunks
   8 oz. seitan, cut in ½" chunks (2½ cups)

If adding lots of different vegetables, start with the longest cooking vegetables first (such as carrots) and finish with the shorter cooking vegetables (such as zucchini).

Add, cover pan and bring to a boil:
   1 cup vegetable stock

If stock does not cover the vegetables halfway, add enough more so that it does. When liquid comes to a boil, turn heat to low and simmer until all vegetables are tender, approximately 20-30 minutes.

Serve in the skillet and let each person help himself. You may also season the stock with miso and serve the stock and vegetables over rice.

Per Serving: Calories: 137, Protein: 21 gm., Carbohydrates: 19 gm., Fat:. 1 gm.

LIGHT SEITAN TEMPURA
Serves 4

To prepare the batter, mix together with a fork and let sit 30 minutes:
**2 cups whole wheat flour
or 1 cup whole wheat flour and 1 cup unbleached white,
corn, or whole wheat pastry flour
2 cups water
2 teaspoons arrowroot
½ teaspoon salt**

Add more water if needed to give the consistency of pancake batter.

Have ready:

8 oz. seitan, cut in 1" cubes	**½ cup broccoli flowers**
½ cup sweet potato slices	**½ cup onion rings**
1 cup parsley sprigs	
approximately 1 quart sesame or safflower oil	

Heat at least 3" of oil in a heavy pan or wok. Oil should be hot enough that a drop of batter sinks to the bottom and immediately rises to the top. Dip each vegetable and seitan piece in batter and fry until golden. Turn and fry on the other side. Remove from oil and drain on brown paper. Add oil between batches so there will be enough for the tempura to float in while frying. Be careful not to fry too many vegetables at one time. Otherwise, the temperature of the oil will be reduced and the vegetables will be soggy and not crisp.

After frying, keep tempura vegetables and seitan hot by placing on a cookie sheet in a low oven. Serve with grated daikon radish and Tamari-Ginger Dip to aid digestion of oil.

*Per Serving with 1 Tablespoon Tamari-Ginger Dip: Calories: 418, Protein: 28 gm.,
Carbohydrates: 52 gm., Fat:. 15 gm.*

TAMARI-GINGER DIP

Grate and squeeze to obtain juice:
1 square inch fresh ginger

Mix together and serve:
¼ cup tamari, ¼ cup water, and the ginger

CHANA MASALA

Serves 4 to 6

Rinse, drain and soak for 8 hours (or overnight):
1 cup chick peas (garbanzo beans) in enough water to cover

Pressure cook chick peas at 15 pounds pressure for 1 hour and 15 minutes in:
2¼ cups water

Let chick peas come down from pressure slowly without cooling in cold water.

Heat in a heavy skillet over a medium flame:
3 Tablespoons corn oil

When hot, add and stir fry for 7-8 minutes or until onions begin to turn dark brown:
½ teaspoon whole cumin seeds
1 medium onion, finely chopped

Turn heat to low and add, mixing and stirring for 2 to 3 minutes:
2 cloves garlic, pressed
½" piece fresh ginger, peeled and grated
1 teaspoon ground coriander
½ teaspoon ground cinnamon
½ teaspoon ground nutmeg
½ teaspoon ground cloves

Add, mix well, cover and let cook for 10 minutes:

the cooked chick peas	**½ teaspoon salt**
8 oz. seitan, cut in ½" cubes	**¼ teaspoon lemon juice**
(2 cups)	**¼ teaspoon cayenne**
1½ cups vegetable stock	
2 Tablespoons tomato paste	
or ½ cup tomato sauce	

Place seitan and chick pea mixture in a serving bowl and garnish with:
1 tomato, cut in cubes
1 medium onion, halved and cut in slivers

Serve with chapatis or brown rice, and a vegetable dish.

Per Serving: Calories: 270, Protein: 23 gm., Carbohydrates: 27 gm., Fat: 9 gm.

SPICY GOLDEN CABBAGE
Serves 4

This is a mildly spiced curry dish. Experiment with the spices (especially the amount) and add other vegetables, such as potatoes, carrots or parsnips.

Warm in a large, heavy skillet over medium heat:
>**2 Tablespoons sesame oil**

When hot, add:
>**1 teaspoon whole cumin seeds**
>**1 teaspoon whole brown mustard seeds**
>**1 teaspoon whole fennel seeds**

When mustard seeds begin to pop, reduce heat, add and sauté for 15 minutes, covered:
>**½ medium cabbage, cut into long shreds**
>**8 oz. seitan, cut into long ¼" thick strips (2 cups)**

Add:
>**1 cup vegetable stock**
>**½ teaspoon salt**
>**¼ teaspoon ground turmeric**
>**⅛ teaspoon cayenne pepper**

Simmer, uncovered, for 15-20 minutes, stirring occasionally.

Serve with chapatis or brown basmati rice. Basmati rice can be found in whole foods and specialty stores. You may enjoy the rich flavor and superior nutritional value of brown basmati over that of white basmati.

Per Serving: Calories: 142, Protein: 20 gm., Carbohydrates: 6 gm., Fat: 7 gm.

CURRIED VEGETABLES
Serves 4

We served this at my sister's wedding reception,
and it was the first dish to disappear.

Purée in a blender:
½ cup vegetable stock
¾" cube fresh ginger, peeled and sliced
3 cloves garlic

Peel and cut into 1" cubes:
3 medium potatoes

Heat in a 3 quart cast iron pot over medium heat:
2 Tablespoons sesame or corn oil

When hot, add:
1 teaspoon whole cumin seeds

After 20 seconds, add:
¼ teaspoon turmeric
⅛ teaspoon black pepper

Pour in the ginger-garlic mixture. Stir until paste thickens slightly.

Add:
the cubed potatoes
8 oz. seitan, cut in ½" cubes (2 cups)
1 cup fresh or frozen green peas
   (if using frozen, add 2 minutes before serving)
½ cup fresh cilantro, chopped
¼ cup brown rice vinegar
½ teaspoon salt

Cover, bring to a boil, lower heat and simmer until potatoes are done, about 20-30 minutes. You can add more vegetable stock if the mixture seems too dry.

Per Serving: Calories: 254, Protein: 18 gm., Carbohydrates: 30 gm., Fat: 7 gm.

SEITAN STROGANOFF

Serves 4

I often serve this dish to people not used to whole foods, as it is sure to please the most discriminating palate. The rich taste of seitan is impressive. My secret is sautéing the onions for at least 20 minutes—the longer, the better. And for all its goodness, this stroganoff is remarkably easy to prepare.

Sauté for 20 minutes over low heat:
> **2 medium onions, thinly sliced**
> **1 green pepper, thinly sliced (optional)**
> **1 Tablespoon vegetable oil**

Add and simmer until seitan is heated thoroughly:
> **2 cups mushrooms, thinly sliced**
> **8 oz. seitan, cut in thin rectangles (2 cups)**
> **¼ cup mirin (rice wine),**
>   **or white wine**

You can add more vegetable stock if the sauce seems too thick. Take off heat and add:
> **½ cup fresh parsley, chopped**
> **¼ cup tahini**

Serve immediately over whole wheat noodles or brown rice.

Per Serving: Calories: 188, Protein: 23 gm., Carbohydrates: 13 gm.,, Fat: 8 gm.,

ORANGE SEITAN

6 Servings

Slices of simmered seitan roll or baked loaf can be used with this subtle sauce.

Prepare and keep warm until ready to serve:
2 cups cooked brown rice

Grate all of the orange zest, being careful not to get the white membrane from:
1 large navel orange

Save the orange to slice for a garnish after the white membrane is pared off.

Place the orange zest in a saucepan with:
1 cup orange juice
1 cup vegetable stock
2 Tablespoons arrowroot
2 Tablespoons tamari
2 Tablespoons honey
⅛ teaspoon crushed red pepper flakes

Whisk and simmer the mixture until thick and bubbly. Remove from heat. If desired, swirl in 1 Tablespoon soy margarine for added richness. Heat by wrapping in plastic and heating in microwave for 2-3 minutes or wrapping in foil and heating 10 minutes in a toaster oven:
2 cups seitan, thinly sliced

Add seitan to sauce. Spread brown rice on a platter. Pour seitan and sauce over the cooked rice and arrange orange slices on top. Garnish with a ring of parsley sprigs

Per Serving: Calories: 191, Protein: 21 gm., Carbohydrates: 31 gm., Fat: 1 gm.

MIRAMAR SEITAN

Makes about 3 cups

*A friend of mine brought this marvelous concoction to a pot luck supper
and it was the food that disappeared first.
An elegant main dish to make the day before a special event.*

Whisk together:
>   1 cup instant gluten flour (vital wheat gluten)
>   1 Tablespoon nutritional yeast (See pg. 18)
>   ½ teaspoon oregano

Mix together and add to dry ingredients all at once, kneading to
work in:
>   ⅔ cup vegetable stock
>   1 Tablespoon tamari
>   1 Tablespoon water
>   1 Tablespoon olive oil

Lay on the bottom of a stock pot:
>   1 (6") strip kombu

Shape the gluten into a log, place in the pot and add:
>   3 cups water
>   1 Tablespoon tamari

Bring liquid to a simmer and cook gluten for 50-60 minutes. Let it
cool in the stock.

Make up a marinade while the gluten cooks by soaking together:
>   ½ cup hot water
>   3 dried shiitake mushroom caps

Let stand for 30 minutes. Mash together in a one-quart bowl:
>   4 cloves garlic, pressed
>   2 Tablespoons oregano

Add to bowl:
>   ¼ cup red wine vinegar
>   ¼ cup olive oil
>   ⅓ cup pitted prunes, cut up
>   2 Tablespoons small capers
>   1 bay leaf

Lift out soaked mushrooms and decant ½ cup of the soaking liquid carefully into a measuring cup; add to marinade. Cut the cooled seitan into ½" cubes and stir into the marinade. Dice the mushrooms and add. Cover the bowl with plastic wrap and microwave on full power for 10 minutes. If you prefer, you can simmer the seitan gently on top of the stove for 30 minutes, adding an extra half cup of liquid, vegetable stock or stock from cooking gluten. Cool and let stand 24 hours or more, stirring once or twice. Remove from refrigerator ahead of time to serve at room temperature. This can be made one or two days ahead.

Per Serving: Calories: 191, Protein: 20 gm., Carbohydrates: 8 gm., Fat: 12 gm.

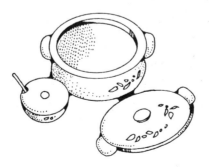

SHEPHERD'S PIE

Serves 6

*As with any pie, it may take a little while to prepare, but it is always worth it.
This pie can be made a day ahead of time, refrigerated and heated to serve;
or it can be frozen, thawed, heated and served.
Children like Shepherd's Pie because of the creamy mashed potatoes.*

Wash and cut into eighths:
8 medium or 12 small red potatoes

Bring to a boil in:
6 cups water
1 teaspoon salt

Cover and let simmer, about 30 minutes.

Drain potatoes, reserving the cooking liquid. Add and mash by hand, in a blender or with an electric mixer 5 minutes until smooth:
2 Tablespoons corn oil
½ cup water or plain soymilk (or enough to make potatoes smooth)

To make filling, parboil until tender (about 10 minutes):
2 carrots, cut into bite-size cubes
1 cup fresh green peas (frozen peas can be used, but must be added later; see below*)
1 potato, cut into bite-size cubes

Remove vegetables from water and cool in a strainer.

Sauté for 5 minutes in a large frying pan over medium heat:
1 teaspoon sesame or safflower oil
1 medium onion, sliced

Add and sauté 5 minutes more:
6 mushrooms, sliced

Add and sauté together about 3-4 minutes:
8 oz. seitan, cut in bite-size pieces (2 cups)
the parboiled vegetables
*1 cup frozen peas, if you are using them instead of fresh peas

Combine in a small bowl:
**2 cups seitan or vegetable stock
or potato water
1 Tablespoon tamari
¼ teaspoon sea salt
¼ teaspoon dried rosemary
¼ teaspoon dried thyme
¼ teaspoon black pepper**

Add to the vegetables and seitan, and simmer 2-3 minutes.

Dissolve together:
**3 Tablespoons arrowroot
3 Tablespoons water**

Add the vegetables and seitan, and stir until slightly thickened. Turn off heat, stir in and mix well:
¼ cup tahini

Preheat the oven to 375°.

To assemble the pie, put the filling in the bottom of a 13" x 9" rectangular pan. Cover with the mashed potatoes and bake uncovered for 30-40 minutes or until potatoes begin to brown.

Per Serving: Calories: 334, Protein: 21 gm., Carbohydrates: 48 gm., Fat: 9 gm.

Variation:

Instead of potatoes try substituting a cauliflower-millet topping.

Pressure cook together for 25 minutes:
**½ head cauliflower
1 cup millet
1½ cups water**

After the pressure has come down completely, remove the cooker lid and add:
**½ cup plain soymilk or water
2 Tablespoons corn oil
1 teaspoon salt**

Mash either by hand, using a blender, or with an electric mixer.

PAPRIKASH ON NOODLES

6 Servings

*Cooking the onions very slowly will lend maximum flavor
to this old country recipe.*

Heat a skillet and add:
1 Tablespoon olive oil

Add and cook slowly over low heat for about 30-40 minutes:
1 large onion, thinly sliced and separated into rings

Onion should gradually become golden in color. Sprinkle with:
1 teaspoon paprika

When soft, remove onions to a warm dish. Mix on a plate:
⅓ cup flour
1 teaspoon paprika
½ teaspoon salt
pinch of cayenne

Cut into ½" cubes and dredge in the flour mixture:
2 cups seitan

If desired shake up seitan and seasoned flour in a small paper bag.
Add to a hot skillet:
1 Tablespoon olive oil

Over medium high heat, lightly brown the floured cubes, stirring
to cook evenly. The pan will seem dry but cubes will still turn color.
Don't worry if some flour is still showing. Mix in a bowl:
1 cup soy yogurt
   or soy sour cream
½ cup vegetable stock
1 Tablespoon arrowroot

Return the onions to the pan, mixing them with the seitan. Pour the
yogurt mixture into the pan, and stir until sauce thickens and
bubbles. Have ready on a platter:
12 oz. medium wide noodles, cooked and drained

Top the noodles with the seitan paprikash and garnish with sprigs
of parsley.

Per Serving: Calories: 245, Protein: 24 gm., Carbohydrates: 29 gm., Fat: 6 gm.

SEITAN MARENGO-STYLE

6 to 8 Servings

A vegetarian version of a French favorite.

Have ready:
4 cups seitan, cut in ½" cubes
4 oz. mushrooms, cut in quarters

Shake up in a small paper bag:
½ cup unbleached flour
1 teaspoon paprika
½ teaspoon salt
⅛ teaspoon black pepper

Put the seitan cubes into the bag and shake well to coat with the seasoned flour. Heat a large skillet and add:
2 Tablespoons olive oil

Put the floured cubes into the hot oil and cook over medium high heat about 10 minutes, turning to brown evenly and shaking pan to keep cubes evenly distributed. Reduce heat if necessary to prevent burning. Put the browned cubes into a casserole dish with a tight fitting cover. If you want to reduce fat grams and calories, you can omit this browning step but it adds a lot of flavor.

Preheat oven to 350°. Add the mushrooms to the hot skillet and cook them a few minutes, stirring to brown evenly. Put mushrooms on top of seitan in casserole. Add:
2 large cloves garlic, cut in thin slivers
1 (16 oz.) can tomatoes, cut in 1" pieces

Cover casserole and bake for 20 minutes. Uncover and bake 20 minutes more. Just before serving sprinkle on top:
2 Tablespoons fresh parsley, minced

Serve with slices of toasted garlic bread.

Per Serving: Calories: 232, Protein: 40 gm., Carbohydrates: 17 gm., Fat: 5 gm.

Hungarian Cabbage Rolls

Serves 6

This old world classic dish takes time to prepare but is well worth the effort. Savor it on a wintery day.

Remove and discard the toughest outer leaves and the hard inner core from:
> **1 large (2½ pounds) head cabbage**

Bring a kettle of water to a boil, drop in cabbage and cook about 5 minutes. Remove cabbage to a colander and lift off several loose leaves. You will probably need to immerse the head into the boiling water a time or two more, until you have 12 soft, flexible leaves. If a leaf seems too raw, drop it into boiling water and blanch for 1 minute. Keep leaves covered with a towel until filling is prepared.

For filling, heat a large skillet or wok, then add:
> **2 Tablespoons olive oil**

Tilt pan to coat with oil and add:
> **2 cloves garlic, minced**
> **1 large onion, chopped small**
> **1 green pepper, diced small**

Cook 5 minutes over moderate heat, stirring occasionally. Add:
> **2 cups ground seitan**

Sprinkle seitan and vegetables with:
> **1 teaspoon oregano**
> **1 teaspoon Quatre Epices (pg. 85)**
> **½ teaspoon salt**

Cook a few minutes more. Remove from heat and stir in:
> **2 cups cooked brown rice**
> **2 Tablespoons tomato paste**
>   **mixed with 2 Tablespoons water**
> **2 Tablespoons fresh parsley, minced**

Taste filling and add a little salt and pepper if needed.

To assemble, cut out the hard white rib from each leaf. Place a scant half cup of filling in center of each leaf, fold in the sides and roll up from the bottom, securing the roll with a toothpick. Lightly oil a 9" x 13" oval baking dish. Drain and rinse:

1 (28 oz.) can sauerkraut.

Arrange kraut on the bottom of the dish. Set rolls on top of sauerkraut. Pour around the rolls:

1 cup vegetable stock

Preheat oven to 350°. To prepare the sauce, puree in a blender:

1 (16 oz.) can tomatoes
¼ cup apricot preserves

Pour sauce over rolls, cover pan tightly and bake for 90 minutes. Rolls can be made ahead and kept overnight in the refrigerator, but bring to room temperature before baking or bake 2 hours if they are cold. Baste with the sauce once during baking. Remove toothpicks before serving and accompany with any sauce remaining in the pan.

Per Serving: Calories: 271, Protein: 24 gm., Carbohydrates: 40 gm., Fat: 5 gm.

QUATRE EPICES

QUATRE EPICES is a mixture of spices much favored by French chefs. You can make up a small amount by mixing together well:

1 teaspoon powdered cloves
1 teaspoon cinnamon
1 teaspoon ground ginger
1 teaspoon nutmeg

Store in a tightly closed glass container.

SAUERKRAUT
AND SAUSAGE CASSEROLE

6 Servings

Flavors will blend and mellow as this bakes.

Have ready:
1 (2 lb.) package sauerkraut
1 recipe SAUSAGE PATTIES, pg. 39
2 medium apples

Preheat oven to 350°. Drain the sauerkraut and rinse to remove excess salt. Arrange in the bottom of a three-quart casserole dish. Peel and slice the apples and arrange with the seitan sausage patties on top of kraut. Pour over:
½ cup vegetable stock or white wine

Sprinkle apples with mace or nutmeg, if desired. Cover casserole and bake for about 45 minutes or until apples are tender. Serve with **OVEN ROASTED POTATO WEDGES**.

Per Serving: Calories: 149, Protein: 21 gm., Carbohydrates: 18 gm., Fat: 3 gm.

OVEN ROASTED
POTATO WEDGES

Scrub:
6 potatoes

Cut each into 6 long pieces and parboil for 10 minutes in a large kettle of boiling water. Preheat oven to 350°. Drain potatoes well, arrange on an oiled baking sheet and brush tops lightly with oil. Bake 40 minutes, turning after 20 minutes. Sprinkle with paprika or salt if desired.

Per Potato: Calories: 121, Protein: 3 gm., Carbohydrates: 26 gm., Fat: 1 gm.

BULGUR PILAF
WITH PINE NUTS

8 Servings

A healthful grain served in a delicious pilaf.

Heat a large, heavy-bottomed saucepan and add:
1 Tablespoon olive oil
1 small yellow onion, diced small
1 cup ground seitan

Cook over medium heat about 5 minutes, stirring once or twice.

Add:
2 cups bulgur
4 cups vegetable stock
½ teaspoon salt (optional)

Partially cover the pan and cook about 15 minutes until bulgur is tender. Turn off heat and fluff with a fork. Cover and let stand 5 minutes, then stir in:
½ cup toasted pine nuts*
or cashews
¼ cup green onions, chopped
2 Tablespoons dried currants
2 Tablespoons fresh parsley, minced
1 teaspoon dried mint leaves

Stir together before adding:
juice of 1 lemon
¼ teaspoon cinnamon

Serve warm or cold.

*Pine nuts can be toasted in 2-3 minutes on top of the stove using a dry skillet and low heat. Shake the pan to toast evenly and watch so they do not brown.

Per Serving: Calories: 377, Protein: 18 gm., Carbohydrates: 70 gm., Fat: 4 gm.

SAUERBRATEN

Serves 6

*This is a special treat to be made several days in advance;
an elegant entrée for a dinner party.*

Mix dry ingredients in a medium bowl:
> 1 cup instant gluten flour (vital wheat gluten)
> 1 Tablespoon nutritional yeast

Combine in a measuring cup:
> ⅔ cup water
> 2 Tablespoons catsup or tomato paste
> 1 Tablespoon tamari.

Combine liquids and gluten flour, kneading to blend. Shape into a
roll and soak in a mixture of:
> 1 cup apple juice
> ½ cup wine vinegar
> ½ cup sliced onion
> 2 cloves garlic, sliced
> 6 whole cloves
> 6 whole peppercorns
> 2 bay leaves

Cover the dish and let stand 1 or 2 days in refrigerator. When ready
to cook, add to marinade:
> 3 cups vegetable stock

Simmer gluten in a heavy sauce pan for 50-60 minutes. Remove
cooked seitan and cool. Slice across the diagonal of the roll to get
broad, thin slices.

To make the sauce, strain the liquid from simmering; there should
be 2 cups. If not, add vegetable stock to make 2 cups. If there is too
much liquid, simmer it slowly in an open pan to reduce. In a
saucepan, whisk:
> 2 Tablespoons brown roux* (See next page)
> 2 cups strained liquid

Simmer until it thickens and bubbles, whisking to keep smooth.

Cook according to package directions:
1 pound broad noodles

When the sauce is bubbly add the slices of seitan, then serve with the noodles.

Per Serving (includes roux): Calories: 251, Protein: 23 gm., Carbohydrates: 36 gm., Fat: 2 gm.

BROWN ROUX

This is usually made on top of the stove and requires a good deal of attention and stirring. It will get browner the longer it cooks. It can be made easily in a microwave without danger of burning.

Heat in a 1-quart measure for 2 minutes at full power:
2 Tablespoons soy margarine

Whisk in and cook 3 minutes at full power, stirring once:
2 Tablespoons unbleached flour

Heat one more minute if you wish it browner.

Should you prefer to make this on top of the stove, whisk together the melted margarine and flour, and cook over medium heat for 4 to 5 minutes, whisking as it cooks and darkens.

To make a gravy, remove from heat to whisk in 2 cups cold liquid, then return to heat and cook until the sauce thickens and bubbles, whisking to keep smooth. To avoid the dreaded lumps in sauces and gravies always add hot roux to a cold liquid or add cold roux to a warm liquid.

QUICK SAUERBRATEN

Serves 4

This recipes is taken from one using kielbasa.
Seitan substitutes well for the meat here.

Sauté in a medium frying pan until transparent:
1 teaspoon oil
2 medium onions, thinly sliced

Stir in:
½ cup naturally fermented beer
or ½ cup vegetable stock
1 lb. sauerkraut, drained
½ cup fresh parsley, chopped

Arrange in a single layer over the sauerkraut:
8 oz. seitan, cut in 2" strips (2 cups)

Immediately lower heat and simmer 20 minutes. Serve as is or arrange seitan around the edge of a serving platter and mound sauerkraut in the center.

Per Serving: Calories: 132, Protein: 22 gm., Carbohydrates: 15 gm., Fat: 2 gm.

CREAMY MUSHROOM SAUCE

6 Servings

This satisfying sauce does wonders for leftover seitan.

Keep warm until ready to serve:
8 oz. seitan, sliced (2 cups)

Heat a skillet and add:
1 Tablespoon safflower oil

Add and cook over medium low heat for about 15 minutes:
1 cup diced onion

Rinse, wipe dry and slice thinly:
4 oz. mushrooms

Add mushrooms to the cooked onions and continue to sauté for 10 minutes, turning mushrooms as they lightly brown. Mix in a small bowl:

2 cups soymilk
2 Tablespoons arrowroot
    or unbleached flour
½ teaspoon salt
¼ teaspoon nutmeg or mace
⅛ teaspoon pepper
    or a few drops hot sauce

Stir milk mixture into the onions and mushrooms, and let sauce thicken, stirring occasionally. Taste and adjust seasonings as needed. Pour over warm seitan slices and serve with mashed potatoes or cooked noodles.

Per Serving: Calories: 118, Protein: 16 gm., Carbohydrates: 9 gm., Fat: 4 gm.

CHOU FARCI

Serves 4

This is a traditional peasant dish, simply prepared and flavored.

Prepare the buckwheat by bringing to a boil in a medium sauce pan:
3 cups water

Cover and simmer over low heat until the liquid has evaporated (about 20-30 minutes):
1 cup vegetable stock
1 cup toasted buckwheat groats
½ teaspoon salt
½ teaspoon thyme

Mince by hand or in a blender:
8 oz. seitan (2 cups)

Preheat oven to 350°. Have ready:
6 medium cabbage leaves, washed

Arrange one cabbage leaf in the bottom of a lidded casserole dish. Sprinkle over several tablespoons of the buckwheat mixture. Top with another cabbage leaf. Repeat until all ingredients are used, ending with a cabbage leaf. Cover the casserole and bake for 40 minutes. Cut like a pie and serve hot and steaming. Serve with soy sour cream or soy yogurt.

Per Serving: Calories: 259, Protein: 25 gm., Carbohydrates: 47 gm., Fat: 2 gm.

COUSCOUS MEDLEY

Serves 4 to 6

This dish is a complete meal.

Soak for at least 8 hours (or overnight) in enough water to cover:
1 cup garbanzo beans (chick peas)
1 (5") strip kombu (optional)

Drain and rinse the beans. Place in a pressure cooker with enough fresh water to cover and cook at 15 pounds pressure for 1 hour. Reduce pressure by placing the cooker in a sinkful of cold water. If you used kombu, cut it into 1" pieces and add it back into the pot.

Add to beans:
1 teaspoon tamari   **½ teaspoon salt**

Cut into 1" chunks:
8 oz. seitan (2½–3 cups)   **1 medium onion**
2 medium potatoes   **½ zucchini**
2 medium carrots   **1 large tomato (optional)**

Layer the vegetable and seitan chunks on top of the beans in the pressure cooker with the zucchini on top. Add more water if you have to to bring the water level halfway up the beans. Add to the beans and pressure cook again for 10-12 minutes:
½ cup vegetable stock

To cook the couscous, bring to a boil in a small saucepan:
2 cups water
1 Tablespoon sesame oil
¼ teaspoon salt

Add:
1 cup couscous

Turn off heat, cover and let sit for 10 minutes. To serve, mound couscous in the center of a large platter. Arrange vegetables, seitan and garbanzo beans on the outside of the platter.

Sprinkle with:
⅓ cup fresh parsley, chopped

Per Serving: Calories: 454, Protein: 34 gm., Carbohydrates: 72 gm., Fat: 4 gm.

MOUSSAKA

Serves 6

*This version of moussaka uses a béchamel sauce that is light,
satisfying and easy to prepare.*

To make the filling, cut into ½" thick slices:
   3 medium eggplants

Place the slices in a large bowl, sprinkle generously with salt and cover with cold water (you'll need to place a plate on top of the slices to keep them under the water). Soak for at least 30 minutes. This helps remove the bitter juices from the eggplants and makes them less acidic. Rinse well and pat dry with a clean towel. Fry the slices in a medium frying pan in:
   ¼ cup olive oil

Drain and set aside.

Sauté in the same pan until transparent:
   1 medium onion, chopped
   3 cloves garlic, pressed
   1 Tablespoon olive oil

Add and sauté for 5 minutes:
   8 oz. seitan, ground or diced (2 cups)

Add:
   1 (14 oz. can) tomatoes, chopped
      or 2-3 medium fresh tomatoes, chopped
   ½ cup vegetable stock
   ¼ teaspoon cinnamon
   ½ cup currants (optional)
   ¼ fresh parsley, chopped

Bring to a boil, lower heat and simmer about 15 minutes, until thickened.

To make the béchamel sauce, heat in a small saucepan:
   ¼ cup toasted sesame oil

Add and cook over medium heat, stirring constantly:
   ½ cup whole wheat pastry flour

When lumps are gone, remove from heat and slowly add:
3 cups plain soymilk or water

Stir until smooth. Bring to a boil over medium heat and reduce to low. Simmer for 10 minutes. Season with salt to taste and add more liquid if necessary.

Preheat the oven to 375°. Layer half the eggplant in the bottom of a 2-quart baking dish. Layer the tomato and seitan filling over the eggplant and finish with a layer of the remaining eggplant. Spread the béchamel sauce over the top. Sprinkle with:
¼ cup fresh parsley, chopped

Bake until sauce is golden brown, about 40 minutes. Allow to cool before slicing.

Per Serving: Calories: 329, Protein: 26 gm., Carbohydrates: 32 gm., Fat: 18 gm.

MARINATED KEBABS

Serves 4

See photo on the cover.

Have ready:
8 oz. seitan, cut into 1" chunks (2½–3 cups)

To prepare marinade, bring to a boil in a medium sauce pan, stirring constantly:
¾ cup vegetable stock
2 teaspoons arrowroot, diluted in 2 teaspoons water
1 teaspoon tamari
1 teaspoon brown rice vinegar

Lower heat and stir until the desired consistency. Marinate the chunks of seitan in this for 1 hour.

Skewer seitan chunks alternately with:
16 cherry tomatoes
1 green pepper, cut in 1" chunks
16 pearl onions
1 red pepper, cut in 1" chunks

Brush with leftover marinade. Grill for 5 to 10 minutes on each side. Brush occasionally with marinade while grilling. Serve over basmati brown rice.

Per Serving: Calories: 121, Protein: 21 gm., Carbohydrates: 15 gm., Fat: 1 gm.

SPICY RED TACOS

Serves 4

We often have tacos when there are leftover vegetables to use, such as carrots, sprouts or broccoli. Simply mince the vegetables and use instead of those listed below. Seitan is also good to use with taco filling packets or prepackaged taco kits. Simply substitute 1 lb. minced seitan for 1 lb. ground beef.

Preheat oven to 350°.

Simmer over medium heat until liquid is evaporated:
8 oz. seitan, finely chopped (2 cups)
½ to 1 cup vegetable stock
1 teaspoon chili powder

Have ready:
1 medium tomato, cubed
1 small onion, minced
4 leaves lettuce, shredded
½ cup soy mozzarella, grated
½ cup salsa (medium or hot, your choice)

Heat in the oven for about 5-10 minutes:
8 taco shells

Working quickly, place 2 taco shells in each of four bowls. Fill first with seitan, then vegetables, cheese and salsa to taste.

Per Serving: Calories: 387, Protein: 30 gm., Carbohydrates: 55 gm., Fat: 9 gm.

ENCHILADAS

Serves 10

*This is a big batch of enchiladas; it's a good dish for company
and any leftovers are delicious when reheated for lunch the next day.*

Have ready:
> **2 packages of large whole wheat tortillas (about 20)**
> **6-8 oz. seitan, ground (1½–2cups)**
> **2 (1 lb.) cans pinto beans, drained**

For the sauce, tear into inch-size pieces:
> **1 large dried anchos pepper**

Warm a dry skillet over medium heat and toast the pepper pieces for 10 minutes, stirring with a wooden spoon so they do not scorch or burn. Put toasted peppers in a blender and set aside. Add to skillet:
> **2 Tablespoons olive oil**
> **¼ cup whole wheat flour**

Cook over medium heat several minutes, stirring continuously.

Stir in:
> **1 Tablespoon chili powder**
> **2 teaspoons cumin powder**
> **½ teaspoon garlic powder**
> **½ teaspoon salt**
> **¼ teaspoon cinnamon**
> **2 cups vegetable stock**

Stir sauce as it thickens. Pour sauce into blender and whiz with the toasted peppers. Gradually add 1 to 2 cups more stock to blender until you have a quart of sauce.

For the filling, heat a clean skillet and add, sautéing until onion is soft:
> **1 Tablespoon olive oil**
> **1 large onion, chopped small**

Add:
> **the ground seitan**
> **1 teaspoon cumin**
> **1 teaspoon chili powder**
> **the drained pintos**

To assemble the enchiladas, cook each tortilla on a hot griddle or heavy skillet 10 seconds on each side, pressing down with a pancake turner if it starts to puff up. Be careful not to burn them. Cover stack of cooked tortillas with a dry towel to keep them flexible.

Preheat oven to 350°. In the bottom of a large baking pan pour:
> **½ cup enchilada sauce**

Tilt pan to spread sauce evenly on bottom. Spoon about ⅓ to ½ cup of filling along one side of each tortilla and roll up snugly. Place side by side in the baking pan, seam side down. Pour remaining sauce over enchiladas. Top with strips of **NUTRITIONAL YEAST "CHEEZ" SAUCE** if desired (see page 109). Bake about 40 minutes until hot and bubbly.

Per Serving: Calories: 246, Protein: 13 gm., Carbohydrates: 39 gm., Fat: 5 gm.

MOLÉ SEITAN

Serves 6

*Molé is a classic Mexican sauce with a bit of a "bite"
and the almost hidden hint of chocolate.*

Have ready:
2 cups seitan at room temperature, thinly sliced

Heat a pan and add, tilting pan to coat bottom:
1 Tablespoon olive oil

Sauté over medium high heat for 5 minutes:
1 medium onion, chopped
3 hot jalapeño peppers, cut up

Add to pan and bring to a simmer:
1 (15 oz.) can tomato purée
or stewed tomatoes
1 cup vegetable stock
½ teaspoon garlic powder
¼ teaspoon allspice
¼ teaspoon cinnamon

When sauce is simmering, add:
1 (1 oz.) square unsweetened chocolate
1 flour tortilla, torn up into inch pieces

The chocolate will melt and the tortilla will dissolve, thickening the
sauce. When the chocolate has melted, pour sauce into a blender or
processor and purée until smooth. Do this in two batches if necessary. Return sauce to pan, add the slices of seitan and heat through
over very low heat. If you like it hotter, add ¼ tsp. red pepper flakes
when you add the tomato purée to the pan.

Per Serving: Calories: 164, Protein: 21 gm., Carbohydrates: 16 gm., Fat 4 gm.

FAJITAS

Makes 6

Sauté in a medium frying pan until soft:
1 medium onion, sliced
1 medium green pepper, sliced
2 Tablespoons vegetable oil

Add and sauté 3-5 minutes more:
8 oz. seitan, cut in strips (2 cups)
1 Tablespoon tamari
1 teaspoon cumin
¼ teaspoon red pepper (optional)

Have ready:
6 large whole wheat tortillas, warmed

Spoon filling down the center of each tortilla and top with salsa. Fold over tortilla and serve.

Per Serving: Calories: 196, Protein: 17 gm., Carbohydrates: 14 gm., Fat: 6 gm.

TAMALE PIE

Serves 6

The combination of cornmeal and fresh corn makes for a very authentic tasting dish. This recipe is well worth the time it takes to prepare, but making the beans or filling ahead of time will make the final assembly easier. Try adding more spices, or experiment with different seasonings, green chilies, and pinto or kidney beans (add an additional cup of water when cooking these beans).

Soak for at least 8 hours (or overnight):
> **1 cup black beans in enough water to cover**
> **1(2") strip kombu (optional)**

Drain and rinse the beans. Place beans and kombu in a pressure cooker with:
> **2 cups fresh water**

Bring to 15 pounds pressure and cook for 40 minutes (lowering heat to keep pressure constant at 15 pounds). Turn off heat and allow to cool, or reduce pressure more quickly by cooling the cooker in a sinkful of cold water.

Add to the beans and simmer about 20-25 minutes:
> **8 oz. seitan, minced (2 cups)**
> **2 ears worth fresh corn, cut from the cob**
> > **or 1½ cups frozen corn**
> **½ green pepper, minced**
> **1 medium onion, chopped**
> **4 teaspoons tamari**
> **2 teaspoons cumin powder**
> **1 teaspoon chili powder**
> **½ teaspoon salt**
> **vegetable stock, as needed to keep beans moist**

For the crust, combine in the following order:
> **1 cup cold water**
> **1½ cups cornmeal**
> **2 teaspoons corn oil**
> **¼ teaspoon salt**

Whisk in 2 cups boiling water. Cover and set aside until thick (about 15-25 minutes).

Preheat oven to 425°. Stir in until the cornmeal is the consistency of thick batter:
   1 cup water

A well-seasoned 10" cast iron skillet is ideal for this dish. If you have one, preheat it in the hot oven for 10 minutes before adding the filling and baking. Otherwise, you can use a well-oiled 8" x 8" baking pan. Pour in half the cornmeal batter, add the filling and pour the remaining batter on top. Bake uncovered for 45 minutes. Let cool 10 minutes and serve.

Per Serving: Calories: 255, Protein: 10 gm., Carbohydrates: 48 gm., Fat: 4 gm.

SPANISH RICE

Serves 6

A simple-to-make, spicy taste treat.

Combine in a 2-quart pan with a tight fitting cover:
1 cup brown rice
2½ cups water
1 (7 oz.) can tomato paste

Cook 35 to 40 minutes until rice is tender, adding more liquid if it begins to look too dry. Sauté over medium heat for 5 minutes:
1 Tablespoon olive oil
1 medium onion, diced
1 medium green pepper, diced

Add to vegetables and stir fry 2 minutes:
1 cup ground seitan
4 green onions, chopped (use most of the green tops)
2 garlic cloves, minced
½ teaspoon basil
½ teaspoon hot red pepper sauce

Stir vegetables into cooked rice, mixing well. If you like it fiery, add a little more hot sauce.

Per Serving: Calories: 116, Protein: 12 gm., Carbohydrates: 15 gm., Fat: 3 gm.

STUFFED GREEN PEPPERS

Serves 8

A real treat at harvest time when peppers are plentiful.

Have ready:
  1 recipe SPANISH RICE, pg. 104

Cut in half lengthwise and remove the seeds from:
  4 large green peppers

Drop pepper halves into a kettle of boiling water and cook 2 minutes. Drain. Fill pepper halves with Spanish Rice and place in a lightly oiled baking pan. Preheat oven to 350°.

Mix in a blender:
  1 (16 oz.) can tomatoes
  2 Tablespoons apricot preserves

Spoon sauce over the stuffed peppers. Bake for 40 minutes, covering peppers with foil for the last 10 minutes.

Per Serving: Calories: 122, Protein: 10 gm., Carbohydrates: 19 gm., Fat: 2 gm.

TOP-OF-STOVE
TORTILLA BAKE

Serves 4

This dish combines seitan with tempeh, a lightly fermented soy food available in the freezer section of most health food stores.

Sauté in a large skillet until transparent:
2 medium onions, minced
1 teaspoon sesame oil

Add and simmer 15 minutes:
8 oz. seitan, thinly sliced (2 cups)
4 oz. tempeh, cut in half lengthwise, then in ½" slices
2 tomatoes, cut in cubes
8 olives, pitted and halved
½ cup vegetable stock

Combine and add to skillet mixture:
1 Tablespoon miso
2 Tablespoon water

Arrange on top of the vegetables in the skillet:
4-8 corn tortillas

Cover, simmer five minutes and serve. If you can't fit all 8 tortillas in the skillet at once, the remaining ones can be served separately at the table. For an alternate method of serving, arrange 4 tortillas in a large ceramic dish. Spoon half the vegetable mixture on top, place the remaining 4 tortillas on top and finish with a layer of vegetables. Garnish with fresh cilantro and cut into squares to serve.

Per Serving: Calories: 335, Protein: 29 gm., Carbohydrates: 47 gm., Fat: 3 gm.

PICADILLO

Serves 8

A zesty dish of South American origin that can be served over hot corn bread or puffed tortillas.

Heat a skillet and add, tilting pan to cover bottom:
1 Tablespoon olive oil

Add to hot oil:
1 cup seitan, ground or finely diced

Sprinkle with:
1 teaspoon cumin
½ teaspoon garlic powder
¼ teaspoon crushed red pepper flakes

Cook a few minutes, stirring to brown evenly. Add:
1 (15 oz.) can red kidney beans, undrained
1 (15 oz.) can stewed tomatoes, puréed
¼ cup raisins

Simmer 10 to 15 minutes. Taste and add a little salt or more red pepper if desired. Optional addition is ¼ cup sliced ripe or stuffed olives. Mixture will be runny. Serve on hot corn bread. If you bake corn bread in a skillet, cut it in 8 wedges. Or bake it in an 8" x 8" pan and cut into 8 squares. Picadillo may also be served over **PUFFED TORTILLAS**.

Sauce Only: Calories: 136, Protein: 12 gm., Carbohydrates: 21 gm., Fat: 2 gm.

PUFFED TORTILLAS

Preheat oven to 450° and dust 2 baking sheets with cornmeal. Place 4 large whole wheat tortillas on each sheet. Bake 4 to 5 minutes until puffed and golden in color. Pour about ½ cup **PICADILLO** over each tortilla to serve.

BASIC PIZZA DOUGH

8 servings

Combine in a mixing bowl:
1 Tablespoon quick-acting yeast
1 teaspoon barley malt syrup
   or sweetener of choice
¼ cup warm water

Let stand for 5 minutes, then stir in:
1 cup warm water
1 Tablespoon olive oil
½ teaspoon oregano
½ teaspoon basil
pinch of salt
2 cups whole wheat flour
2 cups unbleached white flour

Knead the last of the flour in with your hands, adding more as needed so dough is not sticky. Keep kneading for about 4 minutes until smooth and elastic. Place dough in a lightly oiled bowl, turning to coat all sides with oil. Cover with a towel and let rise in a warm place about 1 hour. If it is a cold rainy day, I like to insure a good rise by turning the oven on for 90 seconds, then turning it off and popping the covered bowl of dough into the oven. It will double in size in about 50 minutes. Punch down the risen dough and shape as desired. Dough can be rolled and stretched out to fit a 15"x11" baking sheet with sides pushed up a little, or the dough can be divided into 2 balls and each rolled into a 12" to 14" circle.

Per Serving: Calories: 218, Protein: 7 gm., Carbohydrates: 43 gm., Fat: 2 gm.

Nutritional Yeast "Cheez" Sauce

A tasty non-dairy, no-cholesterol sauce to top casseroles or pizza.

Mix in a 2-quart saucepan:
½ cup nutritional yeast (see pg. 18)
½ cup unbleached flour
½ teaspoon salt

When dry ingredients are well mixed, whisk in:
2 cups water
¼ cup safflower oil

Cook over medium heat, whisking, until sauce thickens and bubbles.

Add:
1 teaspoon wet mustard

Sauce will get thicker as it cools but will thin down again when heated. It will keep several days in a covered container in the refrigerator.

Per 2 Tablespoons: Calories: 32, Protein: 0, Carbohydrates: 2 gm., Fat: 2 gm.

Pizza

8 pieces

The number one kid favorite.

Make up the **Basic Pizza Dough** as directed on page 108. Prepare a 11"x15" baking pan by sprinkling cornmeal on it evenly. Roll, stretch and pat the dough to fit the pan, crimping up at the sides. Or divide the dough into 2 balls and roll each one out into a 12" to 14" circle, placing the rounds on baking sheets. Preheat oven to 425°.

Mix together:
>   1 (8 oz.) can tomato sauce
>   1 teaspoon oregano
>   1 teaspoon basil
>   1 teaspoon fennel seeds
>   ⅛ teaspoon crushed red pepper flakes (optional)

Spread sauce evenly on the dough. Sprinkle on:
>   1 to 2 cups ground seitan
>   or **Pepperoni Seitan** (pg.114), sliced
>   4 oz. mushrooms, thinly sliced
>   ½ cup ripe olives, sliced
>   peppers and onions, chopped (optional)

Top with strips of **Nutritional Yeast "Cheez" Sauce** (pg.109) if desired. Bake pizza for about 20 minutes, until crust is lightly browned on bottom. Serve at once or cool on a wire rack so bottom does not get soggy.

Per Piece: Calories: 402, Protein: 19 gm., Carbohydrates: 55 gm., Fat: 10 gm.

GARDENER'S DELIGHT PIZZA

8 pieces

A colorful mid-summer treat with six garden fresh vegetables.

Follow the directions in the Pizza recipe but top dough instead with:

1 teaspoon oregano
1 teaspoon basil
1 teaspoon fennel seeds

Then arrange on top of dough:

2 tomatoes, peeled, thinly sliced
2 small zucchini, thinly sliced
1 cup broccoli flowers, cut in ½" pieces
   or yellow squash, sliced thinly
1 cup carrots, grated
½ cup red onion, diced
½ cup green pepper, diced

Follow remaining Pizza recipe instructions for seitan toppings and bake.

Per Slice: Calories: 347, Protein: 10 gm., Carbohydrates: 57 gm., Fat: 9 gm.

PIZZA PINWHEELS

24 pinwheels

Kids of all ages like these for snacks or picnic food.
PEPPERONI SEITAN *(pg.114) is good to use.*

Make up the **BASIC PIZZA DOUGH** on page 108 and let it rise until double. Sauté over medium high heat for 5 minutes:

1 Tablespoon olive oil
½ large green pepper, chopped small
1 small onion, diced small

Add to the pan:

1 cup mushrooms, chopped
1 cup ground seitan

Cook a few minutes, sprinkle with:

1 teaspoon oregano
1 teaspoon basil
½ teaspoon salt
¼ teaspoon crushed red pepper flakes (optional)

Stir spices into vegetables, then add:

1 (8 oz.) can tomato sauce

Prepare 2 baking sheets by brushing with oil or dusting with cornmeal. Divide the risen dough into 2 balls. Roll each ball out into a rectangle about 12" long and 7" wide. Spread dough with filling, leaving bare a 1" edge on the long side. Roll up dough like a jelly roll, pressing edges together to seal. Slice each roll into 12 pinwheels about 1" thick and place on baking sheets. Let rise for about 30 minutes. Bake in a 400° preheated oven for 12 to 15 minutes, until lightly browned on top.

Each Pinwheel: Calories: 92, Protein: 2 gm., Carbohydrates: 16 gm., Fat: 1 gm.

FOCACCIA WITH
BLACK OLIVES AND SEITAN

Serves 6 to 8

This is a centuries old recipe for flatbread, traditionally baked on a hearth with various toppings. An excellent accompaniment to a hearty salad.

Make the **BASIC PIZZA DOUGH** on page 108. Roll and stretch it to fit a 15" x 11" pan.

Have ready:
2 cups seitan, cut into 1" thin strips
16 Greek kalamata olives, pitted and cut in strips

Make little slashes across the top of the dough and press the seitan and olive strips in. Cover with a towel and let rise for 1 hour. Preheat oven to 425°. After placing pan in oven, on lowest baking rack, reduce oven heat to 400° and bake about 20 to 25 minutes. Slide out onto a rack to cool and cut into 12 squares. Or dough can be rolled into two circles, topped with the strips, baked and cut into wedges.

Per Serving: Calories: 419, Protein: 29 gm., Carbohydrates: 62 gm., Fat: 3 gm.

FRIED ONION FOCCACIA

Slice thinly 1 large onion and fry in 1 Tablespoon olive oil until soft. Roll out dough and press onions and 1 cup seitan strips into top. Bake as above.

Per Serving: Calories: 391, Protein: 29 gm., Carbohydrates: 63 gm., Fat: 5 gm.

PEPPERONI SEITAN

Makes 12 oz.

Mix well in a bowl:
>**1 cup instant gluten flour (vital wheat gluten)**
>**1 teaspoon garlic powder**
>**1 teaspoon chili powder**
>**1 teaspoon cumin**
>**1 teaspoon paprika**
>**⅛ teaspoon crushed red pepper**

Measure into another bowl:
>**⅔ cup warm water**
>**1 Tablespoon tamari**
>**1 Tablespoon catsup**
>**1 Tablespoon olive oil**

Pour liquids into gluten flour mixture and knead into a smooth log.

Bring to a boil:
>**3 cups water**
>**1 Tablespoon tamari**

Add log and simmer 50 minutes. Cool. Slice thinly to use on pizza, or in sandwiches.

Per Ounce: Calories: 47, Protein: 10 gm., Carbohydrates: 2 gm., Fat: 1 gm.

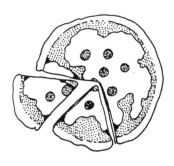

CALZONE PIE

8 wedges

Calzone are Italian-style turnovers made of pizza dough or pastry crust with a savory filling. This large pie takes less time to make and has all the flavors.

Prepare **BASIC PIZZA DOUGH** recipe (pg. 108) and let rise until double in bulk. Divide into two balls, and roll each ball out into a 12" to 14" circle. Dust a baking sheet with cornmeal and place one crust on the sheet. To make the filling, mix and set aside:

2 cups diced seitan
1 (8 oz.) can tomato sauce
1 cup whole kernel corn
1 teaspoon oregano
1 teaspoon basil
1 teaspoon fennel seeds (optional)
⅛ teaspoon crushed red pepper flakes

Sauté for 10 minutes in a hot skillet to soften:

1 Tablespoon olive oil
1 green pepper, chopped
1 medium onion, chopped

Preheat oven to 350°. Add onions and peppers to sauce and spoon onto the crust, leaving about a half inch bare at the edges. Cover with top crust and press edges of the two crusts together, pinching with fingers or pressing with the tines of a fork. Slash crust in a criss-cross near center to allow steam to escape; bake about 20-25 minutes until lightly browned on top and bottom. Serve at once or move to a rack to cool to avoid the bottom crust getting soggy. Cut in wedges to serve.

The more traditional calzone can be made by dividing dough into 8 balls and rolling each ball into an 8" to 10" circle. Spread filling, fold dough over, seal edges, prick top with a fork and bake.

Per Wedge: Calories: 325, Protein: 23 gm., Carbohydrates: 54 gm., Fat: 4 gm.

ROSEMARY GARLIC RING

Serves 6-8

The aroma imparted as it bakes will arouse splendid appetites.

Make up the **BASIC PIZZA DOUGH** on page 108 and let rise until double. Prepare the filling by mixing:

2 cups ground seitan
2 Tablespoons soft soy margarine
2 teaspoons rosemary, crushed
2 cloves garlic, pressed

On a floured surface roll out the dough into a rectangle about 10" x 20". Spread the filling to within an inch of the long edge. Roll up from the long side like a jelly roll, pinching seam. Shape roll into a ring, pressing ends to seal together, and with seam side down place on a lightly oiled baking sheet. With a sharp knife cut slits in the dough at 1" intervals, turning each section slightly on its side. Lightly cover ring with a towel and let rise in a warm place for 40-50 minutes.

Preheat oven to 350°. Bake ring for 25 minutes until done. Check after 15-20 minutes. If ring begins to look too brown, lay a piece of foil on top of it. Remove from baking sheet to a rack or serving platter. If desired, brush top with a little margarine so it glistens. Cut into wedges to serve hot or cold.

Per Serving: Calories: 323, Protein: 20 gm., Carbohydrates: 51 gm., Fat: 3 gm.

BAKED PARMIGIANA

Serves 4

Preheat oven to 350°.

Blend together:
1 cup raw cashews or sunflower seeds
1 cup water
1 (4 oz.) jar pimentos, drained
2 Tablespoons sesame or olive oil
1 Tablespoon sesame seeds
1 clove garlic
½ teaspoon salt

Place in a 2 quart ceramic baking dish:
8 oz. seitan, cut in thin slices lengthwise

Pour sauce over all and bake for 30 minutes. Serve over noodles

This dish can also be prepared by blending all the ingredients, including the seitan, and baking.

Per Serving with Cashews: Calories: 247, Protein: 26 gm., Carbohydrates: 14 gm., Fat: 10

SCAMPI STYLE SEITAN

Serves 6

A medley of great flavors that makes you ask for more.

Have ready:
2 cups seitan, thinly sliced in strips
juice of 2 large lemons (approx. ¼ cup)
4 large garlic cloves, pressed
4 green onions, thinly sliced
2 Tablespoons fresh parsley, minced

All ingredients should be at room temperature. Heat a wok or large skillet. Add and let sizzle:
1 Tablespoon olive oil
1 Tablespoon soy margarine

Add the garlic and onions, and stir fry 1 minute. Stir in the seitan strips and continue to stir fry for 2 minutes until seitan is hot.

Stir in the lemon juice and parsley, remove to a warm serving platter. Garnish with sprigs of parsley, serve with crusty rolls and a big salad.

Per Serving: Calories: 109, Protein: 19 gm., Carbohydrates: 4 gm., Fat: 3 gm.

Scallopine with Peppers

Serves 6

Colorful and full of flavor

Cut into long thin strips:
8 oz. baked gluten loaf or seitan (2 cups)

Slice thinly:
1 large onion

Remove seeds and cut into thin strips 3" long:
1 green bell pepper
1 sweet red pepper

Heat a large skillet, add:
1 Tablespoon olive oil

Over medium high heat fry the strips of seitan and remove to a warm dish. Add to skillet:
1 Tablespoon olive oil

Add slices of onions and peppers, and stir fry 5 minutes over medium high heat until tender but firm. Add to pan:
2 cups vegetable stock

Stir together, then stir into skillet:
1 Tablespoon arrowroot
¼ cup water

Stir mixture until it thickens. Stir in the seitan strips. Serve over hot linguine or buckwheat noodles.

Per Serving: Calories: 107, Protein: 13 gm., Carbohydrates: 7 gm., Fat: 5 gm.

CACCIATORE

Serves 4 to 6

This is especially recommended when it is already suppertime and you have a hungry family waiting for you.

Sauté until carrots are tender:
>   **2 medium carrots**
>   **2 ribs celery**
>   **1 green pepper, sliced**
>   **1 large onion, sliced**
>   **2 cloves garlic, minced**
>   **1 Tablespoon olive oil**

You may add a little water to hasten the cooking process, if you desire.

Add and simmer for 10 minutes:
>   **1 pint tomato sauce, fresh or canned**
>   **8 oz. seitan, cut in ½" strips (2 cups)**
>   **2 Tablespoons fresh basil**
>   **or 1 Tablespoon dried basil**

Mix together and add to tomato and seitan mixture:
>   **2 Tablespoons miso**
>   **2 Tablespoons water**

Turn off heat and mix well. Serve over hot noodles with a fresh salad or steamed greens.

Per Serving: Calories: 171, Protein: 19 gm., Carbohydrates: 23 gm., Fat: 1 gm.

HOMEMADE PASTA

8 servings

Fresh pasta tastes so good it is worth the time it takes to make, especially if you can borrow or buy a pasta machine.

Mix in a small bowl, kneading well with your hand and adding water slowly until dough holds together:

1 cup whole wheat flour
1 cup unbleached white flour
1 teaspoon olive oil
pinch of salt
½ to ¾ cup water

Knead dough about 5 minutes, cover and let stand 20 minutes. Divide into 6 balls; keep dough covered. Pat and stretch one ball into a strip to feed into the pasta machine, following machine directions to achieve thin, wide strips. Let strips dry out on a floured surface until all balls are used. The rolled strips can be cut by hand into 2" widths for lasagne noodles. For other pastas use the machine to cut into ribbons. Let them dry on a rack or a floured surface. Shake off excess flour.

Per Serving: Calories: 105, Protein: 4 gm., Carbohydrates: 21 gm., Fat: 1 gm.

SPINACH PASTA

Squeeze the liquid from ½ cup cooked chopped spinach and knead the spinach into the pasta dough.

COOKING FRESH PASTA

Fresh pasta takes less time to cook than the well-dried store variety. Bring 3 quarts water and dash of salt to a boil. Drop in pasta, stirring if needed to separate noodles. Boil until tender but firm to the bite (al dente). Cooking time will vary; taste a strand to test after 3 to 4 minutes. Wider noodles take several minutes longer. Drain and serve at once. To cool for lasagne or a pasta salad cover with cold water, let stand a few minutes and drain again.

Spaghetti Bolognaise

Serves 4

Sauté for 10 minutes:
- 1 small onion, minced
- 1 Tablespoon olive oil

Add and sauté 5 more minutes:
- ½ cup mushrooms, sliced
- ½ green pepper, minced

Add, cover, and simmer on lowest possible heat for 1 hour:
- 8 oz. seitan, cubed (2 cups)
- ½ lb. tomatoes, fresh or canned
- 4 Tablespoons tomato paste
- ½ teaspoon salt
- ½ teaspoon dried basil
- ½ teaspoon dried oregano

If sauce becomes too dry, add ½ cup vegetable stock.

Cook according to package directions:
- 12 oz. whole wheat spaghetti

Drain and toss gently with sauce. Serve with a green salad and bread.

Per Serving: Calories: 399, Protein: 29 gm., Carbohydrates: 66 gm., Fat: 4 gm.

Pasta Primavera with Sun-Dried Tomatoes

Serves 8

A colorful and fresh tasting main dish.

Combine in a small bowl and let stand 10 minutes:
- ¾ cup boiling water
- ½ cup sun-dried tomatoes

Drain. Slice tomatoes into strips and set aside.

Blanch by cooking for 2 minutes in boiling water:
1 lb. broccoli, cut into flowers

Have ready:
1 medium onion, thinly sliced
2 large cloves garlic, sliced
1 green pepper, cut in thin strips
2 small zucchini, thinly sliced

Heat a large skillet and add:
1 Tablespoon olive oil

When oil is hot sauté the sliced vegetables.

Remove to a large bowl and keep warm. Add to the hot skillet:
1 Tablespoon olive oil

Sauté until lightly browned:
4 oz. mushrooms, sliced
the blanched broccoli flowers

Remove stir fried vegetables to the warm bowl.

Sauté in the hot skillet:
1 Tablespoon olive oil
2 cups seitan, cut in small dice

Sprinkle seitan with:
2 teaspoons oregano
1 teaspoon basil

Into a large kettle of boiling water add a little salt and:
1 lb. linguine

Cook until pasta is tender but firm; drain. Mix the pasta with the tomato strips, the remaining vegetables and the seitan. If desired, pass a little dish of soy parmesan cheese to sprinkle on top.

Per Serving: Calories: 212, Protein: 19 gm., Carbohydrates: 26 gm., Fat: 5 gm.

INDEX

Tofu Cookery $15.95

Ask your store to carry these cookbooks from Book Publishing Company. Or you can order directly by contacting:

Book Publishing Company
P.O. Box 99
Summertown, TN 38483
1-800-695-2241

Please add $2.50
shipping per book

The Tempeh
Cookbook
$10.95

The Uncheese
Cookbook
$11.95

The TVP®
Cookbook
$7.95

The New Farm
Vegetarian Cookbook
$9.95

Mail Order Sources

For instant gluten flour and nutritional yeast:

    The Mail Order Catalog, P.O. Box 180, Summertown, TN 38483 (800) 695-2241, (931) 964-2291 (fax), www.healthy-eating.com, catalog@usit.net

For Asian ingredients:

    Gold Mine Natural Food Company, 1947 30th St., San Diego, CA 92102, (800) 475-FOOD or (619) 234-9711

    Mountain Ark Trading Company, 120 South East Ave., Fayetteville, AR 72701 (800) 643-8909 or (501) 442-7191

    Natural Lifestyles Supplies, 16 Lookout Drive, Ashville NC 28804, (800) 752-2775 or (704) 254-9606

For sea vegetables:

    Mendocino Sea Vegetable Company, P.O. Box 372, Navarro, CA 95463, (707) 895-3741

    Maine Coast Sea Vegetables, Shore Road, Franklin, ME 04634